LARRY WILDE, THE MAN WHO HAS DISSECTED DAFFY DOCTORS AND LIBELLED LOONY LAWYERS, NOW BRINGS YOU THE YUKS OF THE IRISH!

McMilligan and Buckley were hauled into court for fighting. The judge addressed the two Irishmen, "Why don't you settle this case out of court?"

"Yer honor," said Buckley, "that's what we were doin' when the police came and interfered."

Bantam Books by Larry Wilde

THE *Last* OFFICIAL SEX MANIACS JOKE BOOK
THE LARRY WILDE BOOK OF LIMERICKS
THE OFFICIAL LAWYERS JOKE BOOK
THE OFFICIAL DOCTORS JOKE BOOK
More THE OFFICIAL SEX MANIACS JOKE BOOK
THE *Last* OFFICIAL JEWISH JOKE BOOK
     and
THE COMPLETE BOOK OF ETHNIC HUMOR
HOW THE GREAT COMEDY WRITERS CREATE
  LAUGHTER
THE GREAT COMEDIANS TALK ABOUT COMEDY
     also
THE OFFICIAL BEDROOM/BATHROOM JOKE BOOK
More THE OFFICIAL DEMOCRAT/REPUBLICAN
  JOKE BOOK
More THE OFFICIAL SMART KIDS/DUMB PARENTS
  JOKE BOOK
THE OFFICIAL BOOK OF SICK JOKES
More THE OFFICIAL JEWISH/IRISH JOKE BOOK
THE *Last* OFFICIAL ITALIAN JOKE BOOK
THE OFFICIAL CAT LOVERS/DOG LOVERS
  JOKE BOOK
THE OFFICIAL DIRTY JOKE BOOK
THE *Last* OFFICIAL POLISH JOKE BOOK
THE OFFICIAL GOLFERS JOKE BOOK
THE OFFICIAL SMART KIDS/DUMB PARENTS
  JOKE BOOK
THE OFFICIAL RELIGIOUS/NOT SO RELIGIOUS
  JOKE BOOK
THE OFFICIAL DEMOCRAT/REPUBLICAN JOKE BOOK
More THE OFFICIAL POLISH/ITALIAN JOKE BOOK
THE OFFICIAL BLACK FOLKS/WHITE FOLKS
  JOKE BOOK
THE OFFICIAL VIRGINS/SEX MANIACS JOKE BOOK
THE OFFICIAL JEWISH/IRISH JOKE BOOK
THE OFFICIAL POLISH/ITALIAN JOKE BOOK

THE
Last
OFFICIAL
IRISH
JOKE
BOOK

Larry Wilde

BANTAM BOOKS
TORONTO · NEW YORK · LONDON · SYDNEY

THE LAST OFFICIAL IRISH JOKE BOOK

A Bantam Book / March 1983

ISBN 0-553-23032-8

Published simultaneously in the United States and Canada

Bantam Books are published by Bantam Books, Inc. Its trademark,
consisting of the words ''Bantam Books'' and the portrayal of a
rooster, is Registered in U.S. Patent and Trademark Office and in
other countries. Marca Registrada. Bantam Books, Inc., 666 Fifth
Avenue, New York, New York 10103.

PRINTED IN THE UNITED STATES OF AMERICA

O   0 9 8 7 6 5 4 3 2 1

Contents

DEDICATION

For Pat Milligan—Husband, Father, Businessman, Golfer, Shoe Nut and San Jose's most beloved Irishman.

IRISH PRAYER

Take time to work,
  It is the price of success.
Take time to think,
  It is the source of power.
Take time to play,
  It is the secret of perpetual youth.
Take time to read,
  It is the foundation of wisdom.
Take time to be friendly,
  It is the road to happiness.
Take time to love and be loved,
  It is the privilege of the gods.
Take time to share,
  Life is too short to be selfish.
Take time to laugh,
  Laughter is the Music of the Soul.

Introduction

The Sons of Erin have made an immeasurable and enduring contribution to America. They have presented this country with many esteemed leaders in politics, industry, religion, sports, show business and literature. But perhaps the greatest gift to their adopted land is the legendary Irish sense of humor. J. M. Synge, the renowned playwright, once said that "the Irish people comprise a race which has never had to invent comedy—it is a natural asset."

Like all peoples, the Irish are endowed with certain specific character traits that have become part of their heritage. These characteristics, when highlighted and magnified, are the source of big belly laughs. The following is an example of Celtic contradiction, commonly called "Bulls."

"Why do Irishmen always enjoy a good brawl?" asked an American in Dublin.

"Because," answered O'Neill, *"an Irishman is never at peace except when he's fighting."*

The Irish are a supremely sentimental clan. Their emotions can run from the deepest sorrow to the wildest joy. These traits are reflected in their humor. The Irish propensity for quarrel and enormous alcoholic consumption has caused many a comic comment:

The Irish drink harder and fight harder than any other people on earth, and they're proud of it. No wonder they call them the Jolly Green Giants.

And then there is this from Bishop Fulton J. Sheen:

"The reason the Irish fight so often among themselves is that they're always assured of a worthy opponent."

What makes Hibernian humor such a delight is that the jests are for the most part self-deprecating. Like the Jews, Irishmen are not opposed to poking fun at themselves. They do not take offense at disdainful Irish jokes. No matter how taunting, derisive or sarcastic, they seem to revel and take pride in hearing a "Pat and Mike" story. Perhaps it is just their zest for life.

On his 80th birthday, the famous Irish author George Moore was asked to explain how he man-

*aged such a long life. "Easy," he replied, "I
believe it is due to the fact that I never smoked,
drank or touched a girl until I was ten years old."*

Irish drollery is exemplified through some of
its most famous creators. From President Kennedy
to Bing Crosby and Fred Allen, to Oscar Wilde
and George Bernard Shaw. Here's a sample of the
Shavian wit:

*Isadora Duncan is said to have proposed mar-
riage to George Bernard Shaw. She wrote to him:
"With my beauty and your brains we would produce the perfect child."*

*Shaw reportedly wrote back: "Madam, I am
flattered—but suppose it turned out to have my
beauty and your brains?"*

The Irish are well known for their "gift of
gab," that marvelous ability to speak eloquently on
almost any subject. Perhaps that is why so many
have gone into the priesthood and politics. It is also
this superlative skill with the vernacular that has
given notoriety to the terms "sweet talk" and "snow
job." The word "blarney" is now a picturesque
part of American vocabulary. Only an Irishman
could practice it as well as this:

*Quindlen, running for Alderman, was attend-
ing a church picnic to pick up some votes. He
began chatting with a widow who asked him to
guess her age. He hesitated for a moment, so she
countered, "You must have some idea."*

3

"I have several ideas," said the young Irishman smiling. *"The only trouble is that I hesitate over whether to make you ten years younger because of your looks, or ten years older because of your intelligence."*

The Irish also have been known to be vindictive and surly, often taking insult at the slightest provocation. Yet somehow or other the anger always gets sidetracked into humor. Witness this exchange:

After a verbal altercation lasting more than an hour, Wainwright, a British barrister said, "Paddy, how is it that whenever you ask an Irishman a question he always answers with another question?"
"Who told you that?"

Irish Americans—almost 17 million strong—are fiercely proud of their Hibernian heritage. They don't mind boasting of Ireland and its beauty. They do mind what the British have to say about their sacred land. The English enjoy passing around gags that ridicule the Irish; however, the Irish cunningly deflect jibes with boomerangs like this one:

Why are Irish jokes so simple?
So the English can understand them.

You are about to embark on a comical cruise into Celtic cajolery. This volume contains sallies and stories, gags and quips covering every aspect of Irish life—brawling, boozing, courtship, marriage, religion—everything that reflects the remarkable Irish sense of humor.

So, me bucko, if you long for the strains of John McCormack singing *Mother Macree*, the feel of a sturdy shillelagh in your fist, a visit to Ireland to kiss the Blarney Stone, then just mix yourself a merry mug of Irish Coffee and start reading. Here's enough Emerald Isle laughter to make it seem like St. Paddy's Day the whole year long.

LARRY WILDE

Gaelic Gaiety

A Manhattan taxi driver backed into a stationary hot-dog cart and was apprehended immediately by a member of New York's Finest.

"Name?" asked the cop.

"Shawn O'Callaghan," said the cabbie.

"Seems we got the same name."

"Where you from?" asked the taxi owner.

"County Cork."

"Same as me . . ."

The policeman paused with his pen in the air and suddenly said, "Wait a minute, and I'll come back so we can talk about the old country. . . . I want to say something to the fella who ran into the back of your cab."

* * *

Did you hear about the Irishman with two wooden legs whose house caught on fire?

He was burnt to the ground.

* * *

Finnerty was taking his first vacation—a Caribbean cruise.

An hour after putting out to sea, he had to have help finding his cabin on the big ship.

"What was the number?" asked the steward.

"I couldn't tell you," said the Irishman, "but I'd know it because it had a lighthouse outside the porthole."

* * *

Gillhooley showed up at the doctor's office. "What seems to be the trouble?" asked the M.D.

"Two years ago I swallowed two twenty-dollar gold pieces and I want you to do somethin' about them."

"Heavens, man, why didn't you come to me two years ago?"

"Sure, doctor, and I didn't need the money until now."

* * *

During the turn of the century one of the most colorful characters in New York City was an Irish homosexual who did odd jobs for a weekly newspaper. When the old guy retired, they named a street after him. It's called TIME'S QUARE.

* * *

There was an old man of Tralee,
Who was bothered and bit by a flea,
  So he put out the light,
    Saying, "Now he can't bite,
For he'll never be able to see."

*　　*　　*

McCall and Linehan, two beggars, were making camp for the night.

"Yerra, man, what do ya want with that length of drainpipe you're carryin'?" asked McCall.

"I'm goin' to use it for a pillow," said Linehan.

"That'd be as hard as hell."

"Is it a fool you take me for? I'm goin' to stuff it with straw first."

*　　*　　*

Mrs. Shapiro entered the kitchen unexpectedly, and caught Molly the maid with her face and hands unwashed, and a pile of greasy dishes filling the sink. "Goodness!" exclaimed the Jewish woman. "You're pretty dirty, aren't you?"

"Thank you, ma'm," said the Irish girl, "And I'm even prettier clean!"

*　　*　　*

IRISH DRAPERIES

Large Female Breasts

9

Matt Siedman, the handsome City of Hope Fund Raiser, gets howls with this humdinger:

Delaney observed two men cutting down a tree with a crosscut saw. One of the guys was a six-footer, while the other was a shrimp. The Irishman stood watching them for some time, as they pulled the saw backward and forward.

Suddenly he could contain himself no longer. His face flushed with anger. Delaney stepped up to the six-footer and socked him right on the jaw. "You big bully," he shouted. "If the little guy wants the saw, let him have it."

A bunch of the boys were playing poker in the rear of Callahan's saloon. Suddenly, Gilligan jumped up from the card table, white with rage.

"Stop this game," he shouted, "Kincaid is cheatin'!"

"How do you know?"

"He's not playin' the hand I dealt him."

*   *   *

Fogarty and Kinneen passed a Dublin drugstore and saw a sign in the window:

DRINK EGAN'S ELIXIR
IT MAKES YOU YOUNG AGAIN

They decided to try it. Each had a glass of the elixir and after a few minutes Fogarty said, "Do you feel any younger?"

"Not a bit," replied Kinneen.

So they had another drink. "Feelin' any younger?" asked Fogarty.

"No," shrugged Kinneen. "Not at all!"

The pair tossed down another glass of the elixir. In a few minutes Fogarty smiled and said, "It works! I may not look younger, but I've just done somethin' childish. I'll have to change me pants!"

*   *   *

A girl from Belfast name of Alice,
Went and peed on Buckingham Palace.
  She said, "Now this deed,
  Comes from aesthetic need,
And not from a Catholic malice."

      *   *   *

Gallivan and McCord wanted to make some easy money, so they bought a truckload of carrots at forty cents a bunch and they sold the carrots at forty cents a bunch. That night when they counted the proceeds they were amazed to find that they had actually the same amount of money as they started with.

"See," said Gallivan, "I told you we should've bought a bigger truck."

      *   *   *

Keating's relatives were in the habit of dropping by his house for all their meals. One evening he invited the bunch of them in and gave them exceptionally large helpings of pork.

" 'Twas grand, Keating, 'twas grand," said his second-cousin once removed.

"It should've been," answered Keating. "That was none of yer slaughtered meat. That pig met a natural death."

      *   *   *

Did you hear about the Irish Sea Scout?
He went camping and his tent sank.

* * *

Garrett, Dugan and Malone were moving furniture out to their van. While Garrett and Dugan struggled with a huge oak wardrobe, Garrett noticed that Malone was missing.

"Where the devil is Malone? He should be helpin' us with this."

"And so he is," said Dugan. "He's inside holdin' the clothes hangers in place."

* * *

NEWS ITEM

There's a new pill for women now in Ireland. It weighs two tons. They roll it up against the bedroom door, so that the husbands can't get in.

* * *

Thady came running into the barn and shouted to his brother, "Quick, get the shovels. Father's fallen into the manure pit up to his bootlaces."

"Can't he walk out, then?" asked his brother.

" 'Deed he can't. He fell in head first."

* * *

Mr. Barnes stood before a Tipperary audience expressing great pride in his ancestry during his lecture.

"I was born an Englishman," he exclaimed. "I live as an Englishman and I hope to die an Englishman."

"Yerra," came McKern's voice from back of the hall, "have ye no ambition in ye at all?"

*　　*　　*

Two Galway girls met and compared notes on their holidays.

"Where d'ya go, Shauna?"

"I went to Majorca."

"Where's that?"

"I don't know. We flew."

*　　*　　*

Did you hear about the Kilkenny woman who wrote home from Paris saying it was lovely to hear the French pheasants singing the Mayonnaise?

*　　*　　*

A shy maiden of Glenmalure,
Had a mind that was perfectly pure.
　　She fainted away,
　　In a delicate way,
If anyone spoke of manure.

15

Did you hear about an Irish terrorist who switched off the fans of his stolen helicopter because he couldn't stand the draft?

Dick Shrieve, the Sea Ranch golfing gourmet, garners gaffaws with this knee slapper:

O'Flaherty and McGinn were driving through the countryside and noticed that most of the barns had weather vanes in the shape of roosters.

"Say," said O'Flaherty, "can you tell me why they always have roosters on barns and never hens?"

"Sure," replied McGinn. "It's because they'd have too much trouble gettin' the eggs if they put hens away up there!"

* * *

How does an Irishman make love?
He hires a stand-in.

* * *

Mrs. Kilroy was proudly describing the new addition to her art collection. "It's a watercolor," bragged Mrs. Kilroy, "and an authentic masterpiece!"

"Is it now?" exclaimed her neighbor.

"It is," said the Irish woman. "It's even signed by Pablo Masterpiece."

* * *

"An Irishman isn't usually much of a sleeper."
"Why's that?"
"He can get up at the crack of ice."

18

*   *   *

Dublin Customer: Could I try on that dress in the window?

Shop Assistant: I'd rather you tried it on in the changing room.

*   *   *

Eunice went into a drugstore and asked, "Is it possible to disguise castor oil? It's horrid stuff to take!"

"Certainly," said the druggist. At that moment another young lady sat down and ordered a chocolate ice-cream soda. The druggist asked Eunice if she'd like one too. The Irish girl accepted the invitation, and drank it with pleasure.

"Now," said Eunice, "how would you disguise castor oil?"

"Miss," said the druggist, "I just gave you some in the soda."

"Glory be!" she shrieked, "I wanted it for me sister!"

*   *   *

IRISH BEAUTY

A colleen with two black eyes

NEWS ITEM

Several prisoners escaped from a top security prison in Ireland today by using a helicopter. The police announced that they have set up road blocks throughout the province.

*　　*　　*

There was a young rose of Tralee,
Who let herself go on a spree.
　Now she writes to the papers,
　Condemning such capers,
And signs herself, "Mother of Three."

*　　*　　*

Dr. Roger Alexander, the San Diego wizard of gauze, provides patients with this cultured pearl:

Sgt. Muldowney was being examined by the camp doctor. "How long has it been since you had intercourse?" asked the M.D.

The soldier thought, then said, "It must have been around 1940."

"That's an awful long time to deny yourself a perfectly normal practice," said the physician.

"I don't know," said the Irishman. "According to your clock it's only 1955 now."

*　　*　　*

IRISH BANQUET

A potato and a six pack

*   *   *

Costigan and McAdoo played cards every Saturday night for years. When they first came to America from Ireland they had started out as day laborers, digging ditches. But, as the years rolled by, they became successful.

Costigan never forgot his humble beginnings digging ditches with a spade, but McAdoo did and loved to put on airs and brag. This angered Costigan.

One Saturday night at their regular card game, McAdoo bragged, "I wear a suit only four times now, then I give it to the poor. . . . How do you like my gold goblets for beer? . . . My wife has her mink coat lined in ermine. . . ."

Costigan, while dealing the cards, remembered their old days as ditch diggers and said, "Was that a spade you just picked up?"

"It was," said McAdoo. "How did you know it was a spade?"

"Before you picked it up, I saw you spit on your hands."

*   *   *

What do you call an Irishman with half a brain?

Gifted.

Leonard St. Clair, one of the nation's most notable novelists, loves this bit of nonsense:

McGicklin and Brennan were watching a Shriner's parade. "What's it all about?" asked McGicklin.

"Shriners," replied his friend.

"And what might Shriners be?" asked McGicklin.

"They're Masons," said Brennan.

"So it's Masons they are," said McGicklin. "And what the devil are they marchin' for—they get 58 dollars a day!"

IRISH CLUBHOUSE

A Police Station

* * *

Bingham was on trial for armed robbery. The jury came out and the foreman announced, "Not guilty."

"Wonderful," shouted the Irishman. "Does that mean I can keep the money?"

* * *

McMilligan and Buckley were hauled into court for fighting. The judge addressed the two Irishmen, "Why don't you settle this case out of court?"

"Yer Honor," said Buckley, "that's what we were doin' when the police came and interfered."

* * *

Judge: And so this is the fifth person you've knocked down this year.

Brady: Dat's not true, sor. One of them was the same person twice.

* * *

NEWS ITEM

Irish exporters claim that the demand for the Irish digital watch has broken all records.

It is a new type of watch—when you press the button, a little red arrow appears pointing to the nearest saloon.

* * *

Fennessy wasn't feeling quite right so he went to a doctor.

"What seems to be the matter with you?" asked the physician.

"Will ya listen to the nerve of this guy!" shouted the Irishman. "He goes to medical school for ten years, then wants me to make the diagnosis!"

* * *

Dennehy, a recruit in the Irish Army, was complaining to the sergeant about the bread.

"There's nothing wrong with that bread," said the sergeant. "A hundred years ago the people of Ireland would have been thrilled to have bread like that."

"I know," said Dennehy, "but it was fresh then."

* * *

Kernan and Hartley, two laborers, were wandering aimlessly around a construction site. "What're you guys doin'?" asked the foreman.

"We're carryin' these bricks to the other end of the site," replied Kernan.

".What bricks?" he asked them.

"Will you look at that," said one Irishman to the other. "We've forgotten the bricks."

* * *

Millarney got a job on a building site but the foreman was not very satisfied with the amount of work he was doing. One afternoon he found the Irishman digging in a pit. He ordered him out of the hole.

"Now get back in again," he told him. After Millarney had gotten in and out of the pit six or seven times, the Irishman said, "Look, what the hell are you playin' at?"

"That's better," said the foreman. "You're taking more out on your boots than you were throwing out with your shovel."

* * *

A pretty colleen of Kilglass,
Wore intimate garments of brass.
   Pat, one night on the porch,
   With acetylene torch,
Just melted resistance, alas!

* * *

Dunleavy applied for a job at a factory.

"What machines can you operate?" asked the personnel manager.

"Slot and pinball," said the Irishman.

* * *

During their lunch break while working on a New York skyscraper, Donnelly said to Rizzutti, "I know every riddle there is. I'll give you $20 if you can ask me a riddle I can't answer. And if you can't answer one of my riddles, you only have to give me $10."

"It's all right by me," said the Italian. "You try first."

"O.K.," said Donnelly. "What's yellow, has 5,000 arms, 10 legs, 300 eyes, 2 lips, 10 teeth, one of them sticking right down its throat?"

"I don't know. I just don't know," admitted Rizzutti. "Here's your $20. What is it?"

"I don't know either. Here's your $10."

* * *

IRISH CADILLAC

A wheelbarrow

* * *

Gregg Fox, the magnificent Massachusetts home builder makes merry with this brickload of monkey-shines:

Mulvenny was a construction worker. One day the foreman asked him to go to the other end of the lot and bring back a wheelbarrow. A few minutes later Mulvenny returned with two wheelbarrows, one on top of the other.

"What the devil are you doing?" asked the foreman.

"Surely you didn't expect me to carry a wheelbarrow all the way over from the other side?" said the Irishman.

Gaffney was late getting back to the building site after lunch.

"Where the hell you been?" shouted the foreman. "You're an hour late."

"I was only gettin' me hair cut."

"You shouldn't do that on the company's time."

"It grew on the company's time."

"It didn't all grow on the company's time," snapped the foreman.

"Well, I didn't get it all cut."

*　　*　　*

Mrs. Muldoon, the twenty-six-year-old widow, complained to the dairy that the young milkman on the early round disturbed her and woke her up. The dairy manager promised action.

"I don't mind the noise," said the woman, "but I must protest about the way his wire basket tears the bedsheets."

*　　*　　*

Monihan got a job in the Waterford glass factory.

"Monihan," asked the foreman, "did you mark the top of all those crates with the notice 'This side up with care?' "

" 'Deed, I did, Mr. Geehan, and I put it on the bottom as well to make sure."

*　　*　　*

Geany bet Kavanaugh that he could carry a hod of bricks to the top of a fifty-foot building, with Kavanaugh sitting on top of the hod. When near the top, Geany missed his step and nearly sent Kavanaugh tumbling to the ground below. Arriving at the top, Geany said, "Begorrah, I've won the bet."

"Yer have," said Kavanaugh. "But when ya slipped, I was sure I had yer."

*　　*　　*

The widow Payne hauled Haggerty into court for making improper advances.

"Tell me what happened," said Judge Keenan.

"The other night Haggerty came over to dinner," exclaimed the widow, "and after we had our meal, he pulled me over to the couch. In a few minutes he put his arm around me and then he put his hand on it!"

The Magistrate opened his law book and began thumbing the pages. "Hand on it, hand on it . . . hand, hand." Ten minutes later he said, "Mrs. Payne, I can't find anything in the law book against putting a hand on it."

"But your honor . . ."

"Just a minute!" interrupted the Judge. "I'll tell you what to do. Invite him back to dinner. Get him over to the couch again, and this time try to get him to put his foot in it and we'll get him for trespassin'!"

31

How can you recognize a superstitious Irishman?

He won't work during any week that has a Friday in it.

* * *

A young Irish lad named Pat,
With girls would enjoy this and that.
　　He meant to cuddle and kiss
　　When he spoke about "this,"
Just guess what he meant by his "that."

Tipsy Titters

"I drink a pint of Four Roses every night for my insomnia," said McClain.

"Has it helped?"

"No, but now I don't mind staying awake so much."

*   *   *

Slattery was the greatest drinker the village had ever known. One night his wife said to him, "Are you particular where we bury you?"

"If it's all the same to you, darlin', just pour me back into the barrel."

*   *   *

IRISH SAFETY SLOGAN

Don't drink when you drive.
You might hit a bump and spill it.

*   *   *

"What did you get drunk for in the first place?"
"I didn't get drunk in the first place. I got drunk in the last place."

*   *   *

Muleen: I hear that drinkin' is one of your failings.
Bryant: Don't be silly. That's one of the best things I do!
Muleen: I've sworn off drinkin'. Not another drop of booze for me as long as I live!
Bryant: Well, cheer up. Maybe you won't live so long!

*   *   *

"We are now passing the premises of Arthur Guinness, the largest brewery in the world," said the guide to his busload of tourists.
"I'm damned if we are," cried Taggert as he hopped off.

*   *   *

Foyle and McElwain sitting at a bar were completely ossified.

"Do you know what time it is?" asked Foyle.

"Sure," said McElwain.

"Thanks," said Foyle.

*   *   *

Identical twins, dressed exactly the same, stopped in a bar for a drink. Connell staggered up to them and stopped to look at them in puzzlement. Then he ordered another drink.

Finally, one of the twins laughed and said, "Don't get upset. You're really not in such bad shape. We're twins."

The Irishman took another look and said, "All four of you?"

*   *   *

The drunkards of merry Dunleer,
See more than pink rats, people fear.
   Green rabbits, blue bats,
   And six-legged cats,
Leap out of their Guinness and beer.

*   *   *

"I don't really enjoy drinking," said Ahearn.

"Is that the truth?"

"It's just something to pass the time while I'm getting drunk."

Robert Kent, the famous California artist, cracks up cronies with this corker:

Bannon and McNellis had been putting away straight shots of Cutty Sark in a San Francisco bar most of the evening. This was part of the conversation:

"I had the darndest dream last night," said Bannon. "I dreamed that a thousand funny little men were dancing on top of me body. They had on orange caps and green suits and pink boots that curled up in front."

"Yeah," agreed McNellis, "and there was a tinkly little bell on the toe of each of the boots."

"How do you know?" asked Bannon.

"There are a couple of them still sittin' on your shoulder," said McNellis.

In Ireland there's an illegal, homemade brew called poteen. Word has it the stuff is so powerful it can burn holes in steel plates.

After a pint of it, Henehan saw so many animals in his room that he put a sign on his house "Henehan's Zoo." The local constable went to reason with him and was no sooner in than he was offered a glass of the "mountain dew."

When he staggered out thirty minutes later he raised his hand for silence. "I'sh all right, men. The worst's over. He sold me half the elephants."

* * *

IRISH ALCOHOLIC

*Anybody who will drink
with anybody to anybody*

* * *

Kelsey was a chronic alcoholic. The doctor warned him to quit immediately.

"I can't stop just like that," cried Kelsey. "It'll kill me!"

"Hmmm . . . you've got something there," said the physician. "We'll do it gradually. For the next week you can drink four double scotches a day and no more. The following week we'll cut it down to three, and the week after, down to two."

The Irishman staggered out of the office but was back again in a week, higher than a kite.

"What do you think you're doing?" grumbled the M.D. "I told you to cut down to four double scotches a day."

"I did, doc, honeshly," said the drunk.

"Well, how is it that you're in this terrible condition?"

"After I left you last week, I called in on another doctor down the street for a second opinion—and he prescribed the same treatment . . ."

*   *   *

Lenihan stumbled into Bragan's bar and ordered a double shot of Canadian Club. "I'll be happy to be servin' ya," said the owner, "but not 'til I see the color of your cash!"

"Awright," slobbered the Irishman. "I'll tell ya what. I'll bet you a drink that my thing is longer than the cat's tail."

Bragan, amused by the idea, pulled out a ruler and measured the two appendages in question. "Well," said the owner, "the cat beats you by two inches. Now scram, and don't come back until you can pay for your drinks."

"Jush a second," said Lenihan. "Would you mind tellin' me from where you measured the beginnin' of the cat'sh tail?"

"Why, from his behind of course!" said Bragan.

"Ah-hah," smiled the Irishman. "Then would you kin'ly extend t'me the same courtesy?"

McMurphy had fallen into a lake and nearly drowned himself. They pumped him and pummelled him and gave him the kiss of life but it didn't look as if they could revive him.

"How about trying a bit of the hard stuff!" suggested Hogan. "I've a full bottle in me pocket."

Quinlan, giving the mouth-to-mouth resuscitation, barked, "You idjit, hard liquor could finish him off in his state."

The dying man pulled himself up, grabbed the bottle and snorted, "You keep outa this, Quinlan, it ain't *your* whiskey!"

McMurphy then took a big swig, coughed twice and expired.

IRISH DRUNK

A guy you don't like,
who drinks as much as you do

*   *   *

In what month do Irishmen drink the least amount of beer?
February.

*   *   *

O'Hare had been at a cocktail lounge all night and the beer was beginning to take effect. "Where's the little boys' room?" he asked the bartender.

"Go out that door, make a left turn, down the hall, first door on your right."

By mistake, the Irishman turned right and fell down an open elevator shaft.

Another customer rushed over and shouted down, "What happened?"

The Irishman looked up and screamed, "Don't flush it!"

*   *   *

McHillan was thoroughly crocked as firemen pulled him out of the burning bed. "You fool," shouted one of the fire fighters, "that'll teach you to smoke in bed."

"I wasn't smokin' in bed," said the Irishman. "It was on fire when I laid down."

42

*   *   *

McCann, completely blotto, walked into a hotel and registered at the desk. Thirty minutes later he carefully descended the grand stairway and swayed across the lobby to the night clerk.

"Shay, you know that room you gimme? Well I gotta have an ozzer one."

"I'm very sorry, sir," replied the night clerk, "but the fact is, we are somewhat crowded tonight, and as it is getting late, I'm afraid it will be impossible."

"Never the lesh, I insis', I gotta have an ozzer room," demanded McCann.

"What's the matter? Isn't that room I gave you comfortable?"

"Oh, th' room ish perf'ly com'fur'ble. But that ain' th' queshun—I gotta have an ozzer room 'mediately."

"Do you mind telling me just what is wrong with that room I gave you?"

The Irishman leaned over the desk and whispered, "If you mush know the truth, that room you gave me ish on fire!"

*   *   *

"Did you know Shamus is an antique fancier?"

"That's true. I happen to know he loves anything that's aged in wood."

*   *   *

It was three o'clock in the morning. Up to a Houston hotel desk staggered a bedraggled man in a pink negligee.

The night clerk stared at him and inquired, "Is there something I can do for you?"

"Yesh," he said, smelling of corn juice. "Yesh, I wanna be shown up to the secon' floor, room 206."

"Ah, room 206," repeated the clerk. "Why room 206 is occupied. Mr. Brendan J. McDowell of Chicago has that room."

"Thass it. Thass the room."

"Well, I'm sorry, but unless it's very urgent, I'm afraid we couldn't disturb Mr. McDowell at this time of night."

"Lissen. I wanna be shown up to room 206, and I don't want any more sass outa you."

"Perhaps you have a message for the occupant?"

"Neva mind whether I have a messhidge, or not."

"Then will you give me your name?"

"My name ish Brendan J. McDowell of Chicago and I jush fell out o' room 206 about five minutes ago."

McAteer arrived at J.F.K. Airport and wandered about the terminal with tears streaming down his cheeks. An airlines employee asked him if he was already homesick.

"No," replied McAteer. "I've lost all me luggage!"

"How'd that happen?"

"The cork fell out," said the Irishman.

* * *

IRISH WHISKEY

*Makes a man see double
and act single.*

* * *

"Ye must learn to love your enemies, like the good book says," thundered the priest from the pulpit.

Hennessy shouted out, "Oh, I do, I do, Father—me worst enemies are whiskey, cigarettes and women!"

* * *

Did you hear about the Irish woman who outdrank four husbands?

When her fifth husband died she ordered black olives in her martinis for a solid month.

*   *   *

Downey: Shay, officer, where am I?
Policeman: Main, corner of Fifth.
Downey: Never mind the street, just tell me the town.

*   *   *

"What kind of drink does your father like?" asked the teacher.

"Me dad drinks anything," said Sean. "Right now he's under the influence of lacquer."

*   *   *

Caulfield, Kilbane, and McCall wandered into Londonderry pub. Caulfield addressed his friends "If it's all right with you, me buckos, I'll give the orders. Bartender," he shouted, "three pints of Guinness, wid three pints of export bitter from Dublin, and a half bottle of Mountain Dew for chasers. Now—what are *you* two havin?"

*   *   *

"Boyle, why do you drink so much?"

"Well, Oi eat onions to kill the smell of the whiskey, an' Oi have to drink more whiskey to kill the smell of the onions."

*   *   *

Lucy McBain, the magnificent Los Angeles real estate lady, loves this lollapalooza:

McNish, Clendenehy, Lohan and Higgins made careful plans to meet one evening at a midtown bar. After a few hours of their raucous reunion, all four, singing merrily, left for the railway station.

When the train arrived, McNish, Clendenehy and Lohan climbed aboard and the train pulled out with the three men waving and shouting goodbye. Higgins stood on the platform laughing hysterically.

"What the devil are you laughing at?" asked the stationmaster.

"Sure, they were supposed to be seeing *me* off!"

*   *   *

Rafferty with ruddy nose, one hand on hat, the other on his beer belly, climbed aboard the Broadway bus. He wavered and wobbled and finally staggered into the first empty seat. The Irishman flopped down beside Senior Citizen Finkelstein, jostling him slightly. The Jewish man looked over his gold-rimmed spectacles at the sot, and growled, "Why don't you try to be a little more careful when you're sitting down in a public bus?"

"Shay, didj' shee me when I got on board thish bus?"

"Yes," answered the old man. "I couldn't help but notice you."

"D'jever shee me before in your life?"

"No, I can't say that I have."

"Well, 'jever hear anyone call my name?"

"No," said Finkelstein.

" 'Jever hear anyone mention me in conversashun?"

"Of course, I haven't."

"Well then how in hell didja know it was me?"

*   *   *

What is the favorite sport in small Irish towns?
Watching the local alcoholics having delirium tremens.

* * *

McFann and O'Brannigan came out of Sullivan's Saloon sloshed to the gills. As they staggered up the street they came to a dog that was licking his genitals.

"Oh," said McFann, "I wish I could do that!"

"Well," slobbered O'Brannigan, "You better go pet him first so he doesn't bite you."

* * *

TIPPERARY TUNE

She was only a home brewmaker's daughter but men loved her still.

* * *

Dooley had been guzzling with the boys all night. He arrived home in the early hours of the morning wondering how he could get up the stairs to bed without waking his wife. Suddenly an idea struck him.

The Irishman tied all the pots and pans he could find to a piece of string and then proceeded to drag them upstairs. "She'll never hear me with all this noise," he laughed.

* * *

51

Knowles, McGinnis, Lynch and Fisher were returning home late at night from a stag party when they stumbled across the petrified form of Moriarty, the town drunkard. They thought he had died, but a closer look showed that Moriarty was still breathing.

"Let's teach old Moriarty a lesson," said Knowles, the local undertaker. "There's a new grave dug down in the cemetery. We'll put him in an old coffin, lower him down into the grave, and he'll have such a scare when he wakes up in the morning that he'll never touch the poison again."

McGinnis, Lynch and Fisher, beginning to feel slightly pickled by now, agreed. They picked up the unconscious Irishman and lugged him off to the graveyard.

The toolhouse was opened. They fit Moriarty in a half-rotted box and lowered it into the empty grave.

The four pranksters hid behind tombstones and waited for the fun to begin. Finally, six o'clock came and the siren at the town waterworks let out a long, echoing blast.

Suddenly the lid of the coffin heaved up, and the drunken head of Moriarty appeared above the edge of the grave.

"Well, Jaysus help me," exclaimed the Irishman. "Tis the Resurrection Day and I'm the first son-of-a-gun up!"

Deegan stepped daintily out of a Third Avenue booze emporium and hailed a cab. He slowly opened the door, and with great effort got into the back seat. Then he told the driver to drive around the block twenty times. "And get a move on, I'm in a hurry."

*   *   *

O'Dornell was relaxing at the corner saloon when another customer struck up a conversation.

"I guess the greatest drinker I ever saw was McMilligan. Did'ja by chance happen to know him?"

"Know him!" answered O'Dornell, "I should say I did! Why, I got him so drunk one night it took three hotel porters to put me to bed."

Courting Cuties

"Where are you going with that lantern, Mickey?"

"I'm goin' out to meet me girl, Father."

"I didn't take a lantern when I went courtin'."

"I know, Father, but look what you got."

*   *   *

Francis proposed but Joyce refused him point blank.

"But why, Joyce?" he asked.

"If you must know," she replied, "It's because I'm a lesbian."

"But that's no problem, girl," he said. "You can go to your church and I'll go to mine."

*   *   *

55

"Why won't you marry me?" demanded McIntyre, "There isn't anyone else, is there?"

"Oh, Mac," sighed Bonnie, "there must be!"

* * *

An Irish old maid name of May
Once strolled in a park by the bay,
   Where she met a young man
   Who screwed her and ran
Now she goes to the park every day.

* * *

NEWS ITEM

Keohane appeared in a Killarney court yesterday charged with assault against his ex-girlfriend. He had Scotch taped her breasts together. Keohane pleaded not guilty, claiming he was following a well-known practice: "If you can't lick 'em, join 'em."

* * *

Kate: My boyfriend gave me an empty watchcase last night.

Amy: An empty watchcase?

Kate: Yes. He said he's giving me the works tonight.

* * *

Michael Hoolihan was courting Frances Phelan. The young couple sat in the parlor of the girl's house night after night, much to the annoyance of old man Phelan.

One night he couldn't take any more. Standing at the top of the stairs, he yelled down, "What's that young fella doin' here all hours of the night?"

"Why, Dad," said Frances, "Michael was just tellin' me everything that's in his heart!"

"Well, next time," roared Phelan, "just let him tell you what's in his head, and it won't take half as long!"

*   *   *

Quillan kept after a wealthy young widow.

"Biddy, won't you marry me?"

"Can you tell me what's the difference between meself an' Mrs. Kelly's Jersey cow?" asked the woman.

"I don't know."

"Then why not marry the cow?"

*   *   *

Dahill had proposed to Lorene and was being interviewed by his prospective father-in-law.

"Do you think you are earning enough to support a family?" he asked the suitor.

"Yes, sir," replied Dahill, "I'm sure I am."

"Think carefully now," said Lorene's father. "There are twelve of us."

Kathy Vignale, the super United Airlines stewardess, loves this snapper smiler:

Corinne had never married and with each passing year her prospects were getting slimmer.

"Oh Lord," she prayed one night, "I'm not asking anything for myself, but please send my mother a son-in-law."

*　　*　　*

Coyle was quite nervous in his attempt to propose to Sheelagh.

"Eh-h," he said, "I-I-I'd like to ask you a question."

"Yes," said the girl, "what is it?"

"Do you think you could ever marry a man like me?"

"Provided he wasn't too much like you," she answered.

*　　*　　*

CONNEMARA CANTATA

She was only an Irish Bookkeeper's daughter but she'd let anybody make an entry.

*　　*　　*

"I've been told of the bird and the bee,"
Said a sweet little rose of Tralee.
　"Their ways are so strange,
　I could never arrange,
To let anyone try it with me."

*　　*　　*

IRISH QUEER

A fellow who prefers women to drink

*   *   *

On the night before their wedding, Foley was being introduced to Cecelia. Foley was shocked to see that the woman was lame, weighed over two hundred pounds and had only one eye.

Foley took his father into the next room and whispered, "I couldn't marry her. She's not at all suitable."

"You don't have to whisper," said his father. "She's deaf, too."

*   *   *

Killy: The very next time you contradict me I'm going to kiss you.

Milly: You will not.

*   *   *

One evening Seamus and Beatrice were sitting quietly in her father's sittingroom. After an hour or so, Beatrice decided to encourage him by switching off the light. Seamus took the hint and went home.

*   *   *

Bewley sat in Tricia's parlor and began proposing.

"I'm not a wealthy man," he told her, "but I will be soon. I've got a very rich uncle and I'm his only heir. He's a real old man and so ill that he can't live more than a few months."

A few weeks later Tricia became Bewley's aunt.

*　*　*

Grady bought his girlfriend a beautiful ring.

"I wonder if it's valuable?" she asked him.

"I don't know," said the Irishman, "but the fellow I bought it from was a millionaire."

"What was his name?" she asked.

"Woolworth," said Grady.

*　*　*

"Say, Kirk, I heard you were the best man at O'Neil's wedding."

"No, not exactly that. But I wuz as good as any man there. That's no lie!"

*　*　*

The McDuffy girl worked as a maid in the home of the wealthy Berkowitz family. When she became pregnant, Berkowitz sent for the girl's mother.

"Mrs. McDuffy, I'm sure you realize I can't marry your daughter, but I wish to compensate her. I'll settle fifty thousand dollars on the child and give another twenty thousand dollars to your daughter. For yourself, there will be five thousand dollars."

"The blessing of the saints be on you. May the Holy Mother grant you a long life. May the . . . Oh sir, if she has a miscarriage will you give her another chance?"

* * *

A nervous six-footer named Bridget,
Would wriggle and squirm, twitch and fidget,
　　But she knew perfect peace,
　　And a psychic release,
When she found true romance with a midget.

* * *

Did you hear about the Irishman who didn't think much of sex on the TV?
He kept falling off.

* * *

Fagan: Are you going to O'Connor's wedding?
Macay: No wedding for me. My fighting days are over.

* * *

63

IRISHMAN

Somebody who would trample over twelve naked women to reach a bottle of Guinness

Gerry and Katherine were eloping.

"Be careful not to make any noise," he told her, "or you'll wake your father."

"No I won't," said Katherine. "He's holding the ladder."

*   *   *

Did you hear about the Irish nymphomaniac who has to have a man every six months?

*   *   *

McClain was only five feet tall, yet he courted Rosie, the Belle of Belfast, who was six foot three.

One night as they were walking by the old forge he asked for a kiss and Rosie consented. So he stood on an old anvil and gave her a little peck. They strolled on and after a few miles he asked her for another kiss.

"No," she snapped, "I've given you all the kisses you're going to get for tonight."

"In that case," scowled McClain, "I'm not going to carry this anvil one step farther."

*   *   *

Marie Theresa was expecting her first baby. One day her friend Bessie asked, "Do you ever get a craving for fancy exotic food?"

"I do," replied Marie Theresa.

"Like what?" asked Bessie.

"Wedding cake," said the Irish girl.

66

*　　*　　*

There was a young dolly named Molly
Who thought that to frig was folly,
　　Said she, "Your pee-pee
　　Means nothing to me,
But I'll do it just to be jolly."

*　　*　　*

Mulleen sat down and wrote to his former fiance:

Dear Florence:
　Words cannot express how sorry I am that I broke off our engagement. I miss you so much and cannot live without you—can we not start all over again?

Your loving Mulleen

P.S. Congratulations on winning $360,000 in the sweepstake.

*　　*　　*

It was a breach of promise case. The judge said to O'Day, "Did you sleep with Catherine, as the prosecution has alleged?"
　"Not a wink, your honor," said the Irishman grinning. "Not a wink."

*　　*　　*

Theresa Collins, the beauteous Bantam editorial assistant, breaks up buddies with this bauble:

Mary Elizabeth shuffled into the church supporting Theodore, an inebriated groom-to-be. They were standing at the altar rail when the priest approached and said that he would not perform the ceremony.

"Take him away from here," he told Mary Elizabeth, "and bring him back when he is sober."

"But father," she cried, "he won't come when he's sober."

68

* * *

COURTSHIP

*A time during which the Irish girl decides
whether she can do better or not*

* * *

Out in the country Rian went courting Barbara. The young farmer spent hours preparing himself. Dressed in a brown suit, a blue shirt, a red tie, and black Wellingtons, he was sent off by his mother with a dash of holy water on his forehead. Thirty minutes later he returned a nervous wreck.

"Well," said his mother, "did you see Barbara?"

"I did, mother," said the boy, "and if I hadn't hidden behind a haystack, she would have seen me, too."

* * *

Quinn was always terribly shy. One day while out walking on his farm with his girlfriend, Allison, the couple came upon two cattle rubbing noses.

"Sheelah," said Quinn passionately, "I'd love to do that."

"What's stopping you?" said the girl. "They're your own cattle, aren't they?"

* * *

Riordan the welder showed up at the doctor's office with a badly damaged foot.

"What happened to you?" asked the M.D.

"Well, thirty-six years ago I was a young apprentice with Heffernan in Pittsburgh and . . ."

"But about your foot . . . ?"

"This *is* about me foot. I just came over from the old country and I was livin' in his house. Now Hefferman had a daughter more beautiful than an Irish sunset. The first night I was there she came in when I was in bed and asked if I was comfortable and if I wanted anything and I said I didn't.

"The next night she came in when I was in bed and she is wearing her nightgown and she asked me if there was any single thing she could get me or do for me and I told her I was as comfortable as a bug in a rug.

"The next night she came in and the girl hadn't a thing on her and she asked me if she could do anythin' for me and not wantin' to keep her standin' in the cold and she standin' there naked I said there was nothing."

"What the devil has that got to do with your foot?" asked the doctor.

"Sure it was only this morning that I finally thought of what she meant and I was so annoyed with meself that I threw me ten-pound hammer against the wall and it rebounded and broke me ankle."

* * *

Teddy and Shannon had the quickest courtship ever. They met on Tuesday, got engaged on Wednesday, and by Thursday he owed her $350.

* * *

There was a young colleen of Bandon,
Whose feet were too narrow to stand on,
   So she stood on her head,
   'Till the day she was wed,
Renowned for her reckless abandon.

Wedded Whimseys

Soon after the O'Hooley's came back from their honeymoon, the bride cooked her first chicken. When O'Hooley began to carve it he asked, "What did you stuff it with, darlin'?"

"I didn't have to stuff it," she replied. "It wasn't hollow."

*   *   *

Mrs. Bailey opened the front door and the man who had knocked addressed her, "Good morning, Ma'am, would you care to contribute to the Home for Hopeless Alcoholics?"

"You bet," replied the Irish woman, "come back about midnight and you can have my husband."

* * *

As Mrs. Brody headed down the hospital corridor toward her husband's room, she was hailed by the nurse.

"Mr. Brody has made a remarkable recovery. He can get up and go home now."

" 'Deed he can't. Didn't I sell his clothes when you told me he was finished?"

* * *

The Burkes were battling again.

"Oh, if only I had listened to Mother and refused to marry you!" screamed Mrs. Burne.

"What?" roared her husband. "You mean your mother was against our marriage?"

"She most certainly was!"

"Jesus, Mary and Joseph!" groaned the Irishman. "What a terrible injustice I've done to that woman all these years!"

* * *

Dyer: Did you hear about Skelly's bad luck?
Shea: No, what happened?
Dyer: He ran away with my wife.

* * *

It was his bride's birthday and Cogan had invited the neighbors in for a late night surprise party. After their dinner Cogan said, "Why don't you go up and get dressed, and we'll go out to a club to celebrate?"

When she was safely out of sight upstairs, he silently opened the front door and ushered in the guests. As they sat in the darkened livingroom, Mrs. Cogan came down the stairway in a short see-through nightie and in a teasing tone twittered, "Sweetheart, wouldn't you like to come up now— you might be tired when we get home."

* * *

Mrs. Feeney shouted from the kitchen, "Do I hear you spittin' in the vase on the mantelpiece?"

"No," said himself, "but I'm gettin' closer all the time."

* * *

What do you call an Irishman who knows how to control a wife?

A bachelor.

* * *

"My wife eloped with my best friend," announced Archer.

"What was his name?" asked Grimes.

"I don't know," said Archer, "I never met him."

* * *

Woolahan walked in the house at three o'clock in the morning. He was worn out and red-eyed but he snapped wide awake when he found his wife in the livingroom making love to a man on the couch.

Mrs. Woolahan looked at her husband and screamed, ''Where've you been till three A.M., you bum?''

''Who is that man with you?'' demanded Woolahan.

His wife sneered, ''Don't you change the subject.''

*   *   *

A week after their marriage, the Cullens went to their doctor. She waited while her husband went into the office.

"I can't figure it out, Doc," said the Irishman, "but my testicles are turning blue."

The doctor examined him and then asked the wife to step in.

"Are you using the diaphragm that I suggested?" questioned the medical man.

"Yes, I am," she replied.

"What kind of jelly are you using?"

"Grape."

*   *   *

Wife: What's the reason for you draggin' home with lipstick all over your shorts at five o'clock in the morning?

Husband: Breakfast.

*   *   *

"He told me when he married me that he would live on my kisses."

"Isn't that kind of diet a little exhausting?"

"It's not the main course that does it. It's the dessert."

*   *   *

Leary went to his doctor and complained that his sex drive was practically gone and that his wife was driving him crazy about it.

The M.D. handed him a large box of tablets and said, "Take three of these every day. This stuff works wonders."

A month later Leary returned to refill the prescription. "These really are great, doc," said the Irishman. "I've been doin' it three times a night."

"What does your wife say now?"

"How should I know?" he replied. "I ain't been home yet."

* * *

In a national survey recently conducted in Ireland, husbands were asked the question:

"Do you talk to your wife when you are making love?"

50% said they did not.

20% said yes.

25% said sometimes.

4% said they couldn't recall and

1% said only if there was a telephone convenient.

* * *

IRISH FOREPLAY

"Brace yourself, Bridget!"

* * *

Duffy was enjoying a Michelob when suddenly the town fire siren blew two short blasts followed by two long blasts. Soon the roar of the fire engine was heard down the street.

Duffy put his beer down on the bar, wiped his mouth and said, "There goes Engine Company Four and so do I!"

"Hey," said the bartender. "Since when're you a volunteer fireman?"

"Not now nor ever," said the Irishman, rushing out the door. "But my girlfriend's husband is!"

*　　*　　*

Finn: My wife has a terrible habit of stayin' up until one and two o'clock in the mornin'. I can't seem to break her of it.
Keen: What on earth is she doin' at that time?
Finn: Waitin' for me to come home.

*　　*　　*

Flanagan woke up his wife in the middle of the night. "What is it?" she yawned.

"Here's two aspirin and a glass of water."

"What's that for?"

"Your headache, darlin'."

"I don't have a headache," croaked Mrs. Flanagan.

"Good. Let's screw."

*　　*　　*

Betty Brookes, the scintillating Sonoma County socialite tells about the time Pierce stopped at the rectory and demanded to see Father Kielty, the parish priest.

"I have a little problem in the theology," said Pierce. "I want to know if it is right to profit financially from the mistakes of other people."

"Certainly not," retorted the priest, "I'm quite definite on that point."

"In that case," said the Irishman, "how about returnin' the money I paid you for marryin' me to Annie last month."

*   *   *

Wife: You're taking an awfully long time tonight.

Husband: I just can't think of anybody!

*   *   *

Gerald and Katie had just had their seventeenth child so, in desperation, Katie went to the doctor and asked if he could give her a hearing aid.

"A hearing aid?" asked the physician. "How will that help you space your family more effectively?"

"Well," explained Bridget, "I'm a little deaf, so every night when we go to bed Gerald says, 'Would you like to go to sleep or what?' and I always say, 'What?' "

*   *   *

Professor Don Nilsen, the dynamic ASU Humor Conference Director, dazzles students with this dash of drollery:

James and Rosaleen brought sixteen children into the world. Now they were all married but much to the old couple's disappointment, none had provided a grandchild. The whole family gathered for their Christmas dinner, and as they sat down at the table, James announced, "I regret to say I don't see any grandchildren around this table of mine. I want you all to know that I will give 25 thousand dollars to the first couple to present me with a grandchild. We will now say grace."

When he raised his eyes again, he and Rosaleen were all alone at the table.

* * *

The phone rang in the maternity hospital and an excited voice at the other end of the line said, "Send an ambulance quick. Me wife is about to have a baby!"

"Calm down," replied the nurse. "Tell me, is this her first baby?"

"No," said Keefe. "This is her husband Keefe, speakin'."

* * *

Ruth Marks, the radiant New Jersey homemaker tells about the day Mrs. McCarran approached her husband and announced she needed money for a new cradle.

"What's wrong with the one we got?" asked the Irishman.

"We've had fourteen children," she said, "and every one of them has been in the same little cradle, and now it's rickety!"

"All right," agreed McCarran. "Here's some money for a new cradle. But for Pete's sake, this time buy one that's gonna last."

* * *

Vivian: Before we got married you told me you were well off.

Stewart: I was and I didn't know it.

* * *

84

The doctor delivered the child safely and said to Bernard, the father, "The little whipper-snapper only weighs a mere twenty-nine ounces!"

"Well, what would you be expectin'?" said the Irishman, "with me and the missus only wed five weeks?"

*   *   *

Me wife Myrtle's womb has a habit
Of expanding whenever I stab it.
   What's more, me wife Myrtle
   Is so wondrously fertile,
That she's givin' me kids like a rabbit.

*   *   *

Mrs. Doolan was chatting with her daughter-in-law. "I suppose you and Charles," she asked, "are becoming a little concerned about not having any children after being married this long?"

"Oh, yes," she replied sweetly. "We've spent many a sleepless night over it."

*   *   *

"O'Ryan," asked the druggist, "did that mudpack I gave you improve your wife's appearance?"

"It did surely, but it keeps falling off."

*   *   *

*   *   *

O'Morrison and his grandfather were discussing the subject of marriage. "Grandpa, would you get married if you could live your life all over again?"

"I would not," replied the old man. "In fact if they had electric blankets and sliced bread when I was a lad, I never would have married."

*   *   *

One night there was a gas explosion and the Tooleys were sent through the roof and a hundred feet into the air in their double bed. Mrs. Tooley however, was not as upset as she might have been. She said it was the first time in twenty-five years that they had been out together.

*   *   *

Constanza was bragging to McMahan about taking a night course in Adult Education.

"Who is Marconi?" asked the Italian.

"I don't know," said the Irishman.

"He invented the wireless telegraph," said Constanza. "You see you should go to night school like I do. Now, you know who Verrazano is?"

"Built bridges?" said McMahan.

"Nah. He was an explorer in the 1500's," Constanza said. "You should go to night school like I do."

"Okay. I have a question for you," said the Irishman, "Do you know who Paddy Mullanigan is?"

"I don't," admitted the Italian.

"He's the fellow who visits your wife every night when you're at night school," smiled McMahan.

*　　*　　*

A housewife whose name was O'Dare
Sailed on a ship to Kenmare,
　　But this cute little honey
　　Had left home her money
So she screwed the whole crew for her fare.

*　　*　　*

"I've had bad luck with both me wives."

"How's that?"

"The first one ran away with another man and the second one didn't."

*　　*　　*

During a coffee break at the mine, Devlin began raving about how wonderful his wife was, and how happy he was. Finally, one of the men said, "C'mon, now. She's gotta have some faults."

"Well," said the Irishman, "she does have a tendency to use foul language when she's drunk."

*　　*　　*

After only a year of connubial bliss O'Grady sued his wife for divorce. It seems her pubic hair, which was blonde at their marriage, had turned black. The Irishman demanded a divorce on the grounds of fraud.

Mrs. O'Grady stood up in court and as her defense she suddenly took a baseball out of her purse and hit him in the eye with it. She said to the judge, "Look, your Honor, I hit him in the eye with one ball and it's turning black in two minutes. He's been hitting me on the ass with two balls for a year, and complains because it gets a little dark!"

Bourke walked up to O'Higgins and grabbed him by the neck. "You haven't fooled me. I saw you through our curtains, making love to my wife last night, and I clobbered her good and hard when I got home. So there."

"No, you didn't see me," said O'Higgins, "because I was workin' at the plant all night for overtime."

"Begorrah," babbled Bourke, "I hit the poor creature for nothing."

*   *   *

"Haggerty's a born optimist!"
"Why's that?"
"Every year he calls the Marriage Bureau to see if his license has expired."

*   *   *

Since Cecily was going to marry O'Shay for his millions the next day, she decided to have one last fling with Byron, the man she really loved. He had no condom and fearful of pregnancy, they used the scooped-out skin of a liverwurst. During intercourse the casing slipped and couldn't be retrieved.

On her wedding night it came out on her husband's penis. "What's that?" asked O'Shay.

"That's my maidenhead," said Cecily.

"Well, that's the first one I ever saw with a government stamp on it!"

*   *   *

Reilly was complaining to his wife about the size of the household expenses.

"Look at this gas bill," he roared, "You and your unsuccessful suicide attempts!"

*   *   *

Kevin: I'm so upset. I just won a trip around the world for two!
Colin: What's the matter with that?
Kevin: I'm married!

*   *   *

Shelagh was standing in line at the bus stop when she noticed that Mrs. Conway in front of her had earlobes over a foot long. Overcome with curiosity, she asked the woman why her earlobes were in that condition.

"It's because of my husband," said Mrs. Conway. "When we go to bed at night, he likes to nibble my ear."

"So does my husband," said Shelagh, "but I don't have earlobes over a foot long."

"Ah yes," said the woman, "but you don't sleep in twin beds."

*   *   *

"The Coolahan's have just celebrated their tin anniversary."

"Yeah. Twelve years of eating out of cans."

91

*   *   *

Hattan went to the village Justice and demanded a divorce from his wife "because she has such filthy habits."

"What are these habits?" asked the magistrate.

"Oh, I can't tell you," said the Irishman. "It's too filthy to describe!"

"Then I can't grant you a divorce."

"Well, if I must I must," said the Irishman. "I'll tell you. Everytime I go to piss in the sink, it's always full of dirty dishes."

*   *   *

The dong of one Timothy Brable
Was as pliant and long as a cable.
    Each night while he ate,
    This confirmed reprobate
Would screw his wife under the table.

*   *   *

Mulligan was out all night with a dazzling blonde. When he finally arrived home at three A.M. he crept into the bedroom and started to undress. His wife woke up and eyed him suspiciously, then said, "Where's your underwear?"

"My God," he cried, "I've been robbed."

*   *   *

After his burying the man's wife, the undertaker said to McArdle, "What sort of stone would you like me to put on her grave?"

"Just make it a heavy one," said the Irishman.

*   *   *

His wife had been killed in an accident and the police were questioning Finnegan.

"Did she say anything before she died?" asked the sergeant.

"She spoke without interruption for about forty years," said the Irishman.

*   *   *

Mrs. Holligan died on a Sunday and her husband arranged the funeral to be held the following Sunday.

"We always promised we would have a quiet week together," he explained.

*   *   *

After her husband died Mrs. Collins was being consoled by the woman who lived next door.

"I'll miss him terribly," sobbed the widow.

"I know you will," said her neighbor, "but at least from now on you won't be wondering where he is at night."

*   *   *

An Irishman who lived up in Fife
Made love to the corpse of his wife.
   "How could I know, Judge?
   She was cold, did not budge—
Just the same as she'd acted in life."

*   *   *

Kehoe started talking to a stranger at a bar and told of just marrying the greatest woman in the world, telling her name and everything about her.

"Hey," said the stranger, "I used to screw the ass off that bitch behind the pipe organ when she sang in the choir. That girl knows more tricks on a limber prick than a monkey on a rope."

Kehoe said to the bartender, "Hey, Joe, set up a couple of drinks here. Friend of the wife."

*   *   *

Ignatius and Millie were fighting tooth and nail, with the wife receiving blow after blow. After he had knocked her down a dozen times, he found to his horror that the parish priest had entered the house by the back door and was observing the scene. Quickly Ignatius shouted, "Now Millie, will you go to mass?"

*   *   *

"If you don't stop drinking, I'm going to leave you."

"I'll drink to that."

THIS GRAVESTONE IS ERECTED IN MEMORY OF SEAMUS McARDLE WHO WAS ACCIDENTALLY STABBED TO DEATH, AS A TOKEN OF ABIDING AFFECTION BY HIS EVERLOVING WIFE.

* * *

"Those are Eddie's ashes on the mantlepiece," Mary Margaret told a friend.

"I'm sorry to hear he has passed away," said the woman.

"Oh, he hasn't passed away," said the Irishwoman. "He's just too lazy to find an ashtray."

* * *

In a Boston saloon several of the boys were arguing on the subject of who was the greatest man who ever lived. Some claimed it was Napoleon, others De Valera, while a third group supported Shakespeare.

"Gentlemen," said Evans, "the greatest man who ever lived was Michael Aloysius MacGuire."

"Never heard of him," said Cochrane. "Where did you come across him?"

"I never met the man personally," said Evans, "but he was my wife's first husband."

* * *

Mrs. Martinez and Mrs. Muleavy were talking about their aches and pains. "You know how it is," said Mrs. Martinez. "Lots of bills, the kids yelling all the time. When that happens I get the most awful headache, and there's only one cure for it."

"Tell me," requested Mrs. Muleavy, "I get the same headaches."

"I really shouldn't tell, but you're a friend. When I'm like that I encourage my husband to tear off my panties and rape me right on the kitchen floor. It works for me, so maybe you should try it."

"I will," said the Irishwoman. "What time does your husband get home from work?"

* * *

McNally was on his way home when he came upon a woman crying hysterically.

"What's the matter, lady?" he asked.

"Doyle is dead," she sobbed. "Doyle is dead."

A few minutes later he came upon another woman sobbing, "Doyle is dead! Doyle is dead!"

Soon he found another woman crying the same thing. McNally had never seen so many unhappy women. Then, as he approached a railroad crossing he came upon a chilling scene. A train had run over a man and had cut him into pieces. There, on the street next to the body, was his foot-and-a-half-long penis. Several women were standing around crying hysterically, "Doyle is dead. Doyle is dead!"

When McNally arrived home, he said to his wife, "I just saw the damndest thing. A train ran over some guy and cut off his pecker and would you believe it, his prick was eighteen inches long."

"Oh, my God!" screamed his wife. "Doyle is dead!"

* * *

Coming home from the cemetery Mrs. Cudahy sobbed to a friend, "He was a good husband to me. . . . He always hit me with the soft end of the mop."

* * *

HAPPILY MARRIED IRISH COUPLE

A husband with another man's wife

Religious Revelry

"Why," asked the teacher, "did the Presbyterians leave Scotland and settle in Northern Ireland?"

A pupil replied, "So that they could freely practice their religion and force others to do likewise."

*   *   *

Father Flaherty was showing the Protestant minister the new priests' residence.

"You know," said the minister, "this is far better than what my wife and I have at the parsonage."

"That's logical," said Father Flaherty. "Protestant ministers have better halves and Catholic priests have better quarters."

*   *   *

The family gathered around the baptismal font and the ceremony commenced.

"And now," said the priest, "what name are you giving the child?"

"Peter Xavier Timothy Eamonn Richard Albert Daniel Sean Paxton," announced the godmother proudly.

The priest turned to the altar boy. "Quick, get more Holy Water."

*   *   *

IRISH ATHEIST

A man who goes about wishing to God he could believe in God

*   *   *

An American tourist visiting Belfast became quite disturbed when the Irish civil war erupted in some bombings. He stopped a passerby and asked, "Say, what does a man do around here if he's an atheist?"

"Well, me boy, that all depends on whether he's a Protestant atheist or a Catholic atheist."

*   *   *

Father Donovan had been revealing his innermost feelings about sex to a psychiatrist. "Perhaps when these erotic thoughts enter your mind," advised the shrink, "you should simply take a cold shower."

"I've taken so many cold showers to fight temptation," said the priest, "that every time it rains, I get an erection."

*　　*　　*

Cooney, completely ossified, stumbled out of a saloon and into a Catholic church. He spotted the confessional and tiptoed inside. The priest thought he heard someone and tapped on the partition wall.

"Forget it, buddy!" said Cooney. "There's no paper in here, either."

*　　*　　*

Father Coonan had finished the Sunday morning service and was shouting at his parishioners. In the middle of the sermon he called out, "Stand up, all ye who prefer sin!"

Quillan, who had been half asleep, jumped to his feet.

"Do you prefer sin?" roared the priest.

"Oh, I'm sorry! I thought you said 'gin.' "

*　　*　　*

A Protestant friend of Terence Cardinal Cooke presented him with a ticket to the show *Jesus Christ Superstar*.

Next day the cardinal was asked by his friend, "Well, how did you like it?"

"It wasn't as good as the Book."

*   *   *

Harwin, a Protestant roofing contractor, was repairing a roof of a Catholic church. While looking down, Harwin spotted old Mrs. Coogan on her knees praying. As a practical joke he roared, "This is Jesus. Your prayers will be answered."

Mrs. Coogan kept right on praying.

Again, Harwin intoned, "This is Jesus. Your prayers will be answered."

"Will you shut up," said the Irish woman, "I'm talkin' to yer mother."

*   *   *

A visiting archbishop had just preached an eloquent sermon on the beauties of married life. As they came out of church, Mrs. Purdy said to her friend, "Sure 'tis a fine sermon his reverence is after givin' us."

"Indeed it is," said the other Irish woman, "and I wish I knew as little about the subject as he does!"

*   *   *

Mrs. Redmond went into the confession box and was about to start when she noticed an unfamiliar face behind the shutter.

"You're not Father Donlon. What are you doing there?"

"I'm the furniture polisher, M'am."

"Well, where is Father Donlon?"

"I couldn't tell you, but if he heard anything like the stories I've been listening to, he's gone for the police."

* * *

Kellem returned to his hometown after many years in the big city.

"I hope," said his parish priest, "that you have been loyal to your faith while you've been away?"

"Indeed, Father, I have. I lied, I fought, I cursed, I robbed and I had women, but not for one moment did I forget the religion I was brought up in."

* * *

"Are you a regular churchgoer, O'Hara?"

"None better, Father. I go every Easter."

Father Fryme, who was visiting with old Mrs. Crandall, admired her parrot.

"Pull his right leg," said Mrs. Crandall.

The priest did as she asked and stood back in amazement as the parrot intoned the *Lord's Prayer*.

"Now pull his left leg," said the old lady.

This time the parrot recited the *Rosary*.

"What will happen if I pull both legs together?" joked the priest.

"I'll fall on my ass, you dummy," said the parrot.

*　　*　　*

Father Reardon was giving a sermon one morning in his church when he inadvertently began swinging his beads. The more he swung the beads the more his parishioners became mesmerized by the motion. Finally, when the priest mentioned giving from the heart, the collection plates were filled to overflowing.

Father Reardon, pleased with his accomplishment, decided the following Sunday to swing his beads while delivering his sermon. Once again the congregation became hypnotized and gave all they had come to church with.

The following week, an accident happened. While the priest gave his sermon and swung his beads they hit the side of the lectern and broke. The tiny beads splashed all over the church. The shock of it caused Father Reardon to exclaim, "Oh, shit!"

It took three weeks to clean up the church.

*　　*　　*

Reverend Quillan, a Protestant minister, received a letter from a youth asking "Is it possible to lead a good Christian life in Chicago on 100 dollars a week?"

"My dear boy," replied the minister, "that's about all you can do."

*   *   *

The Cardinal died but he was allowed to return to the Vatican one hour to speak to the Irish Bishops.

"What is God like?" they asked. "Is he like the paintings of him? Do tell us."

"Well," answered the Cardinal, "to start with—she's black. . . ."

*   *   *

Comedians get big boffs when they tell religious stories. It is human nature to poke fun at taboos, traditions and pomposity, and audiences love hearing jokes about the church. Here are some beauts:

Popular comic Joe Bingo tells about Riley stumbling out of a saloon and bumping into Father Moody. "You're intoxicated," said the priest.

"I'm glad to see you, Father," said the Irishman.

"Why is that?"

"I want to ask you what causes arthritis?"

"Arthritis is caused by drinking to excess," scowled the priest, "carousing late at night, chasing around with wild women and getting into all kinds of trouble. Why do you ask?"

"I read in this morning's paper that the Pope had it."

107

* * *

Funny man Billy Blair Cunningham cracks up crowds with this corker:

Elderly Father Hanlon telephoned the police station and said, "There's a dead jackass on the front lawn. Send down some young cops to drag it away."

"Well, Father," said the desk sergeant, "isn't it the church's duty to bury the dead?"

"It is," replied the priest, "but it is also our duty to notify the next of kin!"

* * *

Tom Dreeson, the dynamite comic from Chicago, destroys audiences with these classic comments on his Catholic background:

"When I was growing up, my Mom wanted me to become a priest, which I think is a tough occupation. Can you imagine giving up your sex life and then once a week people come in to tell you all the highlights of theirs?"

"But I love to go back home and see the nuns again. It's so different now because they don't wear the habit anymore. They wear civilian clothes, although they have a very strict dress code. They have to wear a plain dress with a Cross-Your-Heart bra and No-Nonsense pantyhose."

108

*　　*　　*

Boston's contribution to the laugh maker fraternity, Billy Kelly, convulses audiences with these casual comedic observations:

"My family was the only Irish family in my neighborhood. I was a choir boy until I was thirty-three years old.

"We had a very small parish; our bingo board had only eleven numbers.

"We did all right, though. Father O'Mally, our pastor, used to holler the numbers out in Latin so the Protestants wouldn't win."

*　　*　　*

A hapless church tenor was Horace,
Whose skin was so terribly porous,
　　Sometimes in the choir
　　He'd start to perspire,
And nearly drown out the whole chorus.

*　　*　　*

Father Conway was haranguing his parishioners: "The drink has killed millions, it rots their stomachs and they die in agony. Smoking has killed millions. It coats their lungs and they too die in agony. Overeating and consorting with loose women have also killed millions. . . ."

"S'cuse me, Father," roared Regan from the back, "but what is it that kills the people who live right?"

*   *   *

On her way home to the convent Sister Margaret Theresa took a short cut through the park and was attacked and raped several times by a young man.

The Mother Superior, hearing of the terrible incident, hurried to the hospital and met with the doctor on duty. "Mercy! How is poor Sister Margaret Theresa?"

"She's doing fine," said the M.D. "They should be through with the plastic surgery in a few hours."

"What?" exclaimed Mother Superior. "Why in the Holy Mother's name would she be needin' plastic surgery?"

"We're trying to get the smile off her face!"

*   *   *

Sister Agnes and Sister Mary were chatting one evening. "What do you miss the most being a nun?" asked Sister Agnes.

"I miss my little drink," said Sister Mary.

"Let's sneak out tonight and get one."

That night the nuns tiptoed from the nunnery and headed across an empty field. As they crawled along the ground under some barbed wire Sister Mary said, "I feel like a Marine."

"Don't be silly," replied Sister Agnes. "There isn't a Marine around for miles."

*   *   *

Father Dennis called in one of the sisters for a chat. "What would you have been if you hadn't become a nun?" he asked.

"A prostitute," replied the nun.

The priest almost had a heart attack. He pulled himself together and repeated the question.

"A prostitute," answered the sister again.

"Oh, thank the good Lord," sighed Father Dennis. "I thought you said a Protestant."

*　　*　　*

Katherine, a novice, was warned by the Mother Superior to be careful when helping ailing Father Purcell take his bath. "He's getting on in years, but is still surprisingly dangerous," she explained. "It's important to keep your eyes above his waist, or he becomes overly excited."

Later, the older nun called Katherine into her office. "Tell me," she inquired, "how did things go?"

"I-I'm afraid that I did look down, Mother," blushed the young novice, "and that Father Purcell saw me do it. And then he seemed to grow younger and younger and he said that it was the key to heaven and that I had the lock—and, w-well, I let him see if it would fit."

"Why, the old scoundrel!" exclaimed the Mother Superior. "All those years he's been telling me that it was Gabriel's trumpet."

*　　*　　*

Different women react differently when leaving their lovers the morning after. Here are comments from ladies of various nationalities:

The English girl departs casually and chirps "By jove, that was jolly good."

The American girl kisses her date and says "Wow, you great big hunk of wunnerful manhood—Grrrr."

The French girl lingers, gazing at her man and purrs "*Ooh la la, my chéri.* Can we start again soon—mmm?"

The Irish girl grabs her raincoat, headscarf, beads and prayerbook; rushes out the door shouting "Good God! It's half-past seven. I'll be late for Mass."

Dave Allen, the brilliant British TV funnyman, tells this beauty:

Harrigan was about to enter a Dublin pub, when he was accosted by a nun. "How dare you drink that awful poison," she admonished. "You should be ashamed of yourself. Liquor is the curse of mankind. It is nothing but foul tasting. . . ."

"Now hold on, sister," stopped Harrigan. "A bit of the stuff never hurt anyone. A couple of drinks and I feel like a new man. You don't know what you're talkin' about because you've never tasted the stuff. You shouldn't be talkin' against something you've never even tried. Now I'm goin' to buy you a drink and then you can offer your opinion."

"What kind should I be havin?"

"Gin."

"All right, then. But have them put it in a cup so no one can tell."

Harrigan walked up to the bar and said, "Give me a scotch and a double gin in a cup!"

"Oh, no," said the barkeep. "Is that old nun out there again?"

*　　*　　*

Penelope, a pretty Boston bank teller, went to confession and told the priest that she had had sexual relations on five occasions. He told her to say fifty *Hail Marys* as penance.

Three months later, Penny moved to Chicago and went once more to confession. This time she again admitted to having engaged in the sex act five times.

"As penance," intoned the priest, "say ten *Hail Marys*!"

"Thank you, Father," she said, "but why only ten *Hail Marys*? I confessed to the same thing in Boston and was told to say fifty of them."

"That may be so," replied the priest, "but what do they know about screwing in Boston?"

*   *   *

Little Douglas had been sitting close to the confession box door for a long time before Father Delaney noticed him.

"Have you been listening to confessions all evening?" blustered the priest.

"Oh, no, Father. I'm only here since the girl who went down on the sailor came out."

*   *   *

Elizabeth was terribly shy and found it difficult to confess. The priest offered his help. "Did he do this?" he asked, kissing her.

"Yes, Father, and worse."

"You mean he did this?" he said, massaging her breasts.

"Yes, Father, and worse."

Then he had intercourse with her, "You mean that's what he did?"

"Yes, Father, and worse, too!"

"What worse could he do?"

"He gave me the clap, Father!"

115

*   *   *

The Irish missionary was preaching to the African tribe.

"And I say to you that you must love your fellowmen!"

"*Googoolumba!*" shrieked the natives.

"White man and black man must learn to co-operate."

"*Googoolumba!*" chanted the crowd.

The missionary was delighted and told the chief how pleased he was with the reception.

"Me happy, O man of Ireland," said the chief. "But be careful as we pass my cattle that you do not step into the *GooGoolumba!*"

*   *   *

Flaherty decided to become a Trappist Monk. The Abbot Augustine in charge welcomed him and said, "We are a very strict order. You must live a life of severe penitential discipline. You will be allowed to speak only two words every five years."

Flaherty agreed and at the end of the fifth year he entered the brother's office. "You've been a good monk and I will allow you to speak two words."

"Hard bed," said Flaherty.

"I know, my son, but that's part of the discipline. Go now, and fulfill your duties."

Five years later, Flaherty was back. "You now may speak your two words," said Augustine.

"Bad food," said Flaherty.

116

"Yes, my son, but we are a poor monastery. Go about your work now."

At last, another five long years passed and once again Flaherty stood before the abbot. "You may speak, my son."

Flaherty exclaimed, "I quit!"

"That's perfectly all right!" said the abbot. "You've done nothing but complain since the moment you got here!"

Bumbling Bulls

The unique Irish sense of humor has produced a special formula for evoking laughter called a "bull." At best a bull can be defined as an absurd contradictory statement which is itself a paradox. Almost always it is a grotesque or ludicrous verbal blunder.

There are conflicting accounts as to the origin of these bulls. One acceptable explanation lays their creation at the feet of Obadiah Bull, an Irish lawyer who is said to have practiced law during the reign of Henry VII.

Attorney Bull appeared in court one day and during his opening remarks said, "His brother and

sister are very much alike, especially his sister."
The spectators looked at each other blankly and
then burst out in gales of laughter. Later in the day
Bull commented, "The only way to prevent what's
past is to prevent it before it happens." This sent
courtroom spectators scurrying home to tell their
neighbors and friends and insured comedic immor-
tality for Lawyer Bull.

From then on every paradoxical ludicrous ut-
terance became known as a bull and the Irish seem
to be responsible for most of them. Here are some
classics:

*　　*　　*

"What time is it?" asked Lanahan.
"I don't know exactly, but it's not four
o'clock," answered Ginty, "because I told my
wife I'd be home by four o'clock and I'm not home
yet."

*　　*　　*

Captivating Katharine Gates, the Hancock Park
homemaker, tells about the two Irish ladies meeting
in the supermarket:
"I hear that your husband had a post-mortem
operation," said Mrs. McGill.
"Yes," replied Mrs. Cleary, "but not until
after he was dead. If only they had done it a bit
earlier it might have saved his life."

*　　*　　*

McGuire the politician began his speech: "There is something I want to get off me chest today that has been hanging over me head for weeks, and I'll be glad to put it behind me before we come to the end."

* * *

ROAD SIGN IN CORK

When this sign is under water the road is closed for traffic

* * *

Beamish stood up from the breakfast table and announced to his family, "Has anyone here seen me vest, then?"

"Shure and you have the thing on, you fool," said his wife.

"Well, thanks anyway because I'd have gone without it if you hadn't happened to notice."

* * *

Glendora: I've broken my glasses. Will I have to be examined all over again?

Dr. Carey: No, just your eyes.

*   *   *

Daniel and Teddy were traveling down to London on their motorbikes. Daniel had not been to the big city before and Teddy had. "Listen," said Daniel. "Seeing as you know the way and I don't, Teddy, you go on ahead and I will follow on in front."

*   *   *

"Sure," said McGrath, "here in Ireland we could have the best weather there is anywhere in the world if the climate didn't spoil it."

*   *   *

"Folan, listen to me. If McGowan comes back before I return tell him I'll meet him at 4 o'clock."

"Sure I will do that, sor, but what will I tell him if he doesn't come?"

*   *   *

Professor Hogarty was lecturing about his travels in foreign countries. "I came across a strange custom among the Chinese," he told his audience. "If a rich man was condemned to death, he could save his life by paying somebody to die in his place. Many of the poor people made their living by acting as substitutes in this way."

McGuffy fell fifty feet and was asked if the fall had hurt him. "No," he said, " 'twas the abrupt stop." He thought for a moment and then said, "I was actually rather lucky that the ground broke my fall."

* * *

Gannaway, the eminent Dublin archaeologist, was giving a lecture at Ohio University.

"Some of the cities of the past," he explained, "have vanished so completely that it's doubtful if some of them existed at all."

* * *

Feeney bought his wife a pair of rubber gloves. When he asked her how she was getting on with them, she said, "They're really very good."

"When you've got them on, sure, and you can wash your hands without getting them wet."

* * *

Dugan and Nugent were sitting on a park bench discussing politics. "All right, then," said Dugan. "If Henry Ford and Gerald Ford aren't the same person, how come you don't ever see them together?"

* * *

Ray Fisher, the famous Florida photographer, fancies this fit of frivolity:

There was an accident at the construction site. Couglan ran to where Mooney lay in a pile of rubble. "Are ye dead after such a nasty fall?" he said.

"That I am indeed," said Mooney.

"Faith and you're such a liar I don't know if to believe you or not, bejabbers."

"That proves I'm dead, ye idjit!" said Mooney, raising himself. "If I wuz alive you'd not be callin' me a liar to me dead face."

"Happy are the parents that have no children."
—Obadiah Bull

*   *   *

Two lawyers standing before Judge McMannus got into a fierce argument.

At last one lawyer lost his temper and shouted at his opponent.

"Sir, you are the biggest fool that I have had the misfortune to set eyes on."

"Order, order," said McMannus. "You seem to forget that I am in the room."

*   *   *

The defendant had been found guilty and Judge Dillon was furious. "Young man," he roared, "any fool who maliciously sets fire to a barn to burn it in addition to burning a stable full of horses ought to be kicked to death by an imbecile jackass, and I'd like to be the one to do it."

*   *   *

Killian the auctioneer stood up before the crowd and shouted, "The highest bidder will be deemed to be the person or persons nominated as the buyer or buyers unless someone else offers more. . . ."

*   *   *

Dempsey came home and almost immediately began berating his wife.

"Did you ever take time to think if you've got a brain?"

"Certainly not," retorted the Missus. "Such a thing would never enter my head."

* * *

NOTICE IN SOUTH BOSTON

House To Let forever—
Or longer if required.

* * *

"Was it crowded down at the Union Meeting?"

"I'll say. When they stood up to sing 'God Bless America' there wasn't an empty seat in the whole sacred building."

* * *

Clancy approached Tornetta, his next-door neighbor. "Hey, I got a heavy date tonight and I'd like to borrow your car."

"You borrowed it last night and didn't bring it back," said Tornetta.

"That's too bad," said Clancy. "I wanted to borrow it again tonight."

* * *

Moran: Does he stutter all the time?
Nolan: No, only when he talks.

*   *   *

O'Donovan ran into an old friend. "I'm sorry I didn't recognize you," he said, "but you see I've changed a lot."

*   *   *

"Hey, I'm glad to see you," Denahy told his old pal Logan. "There's a rumor going 'round that you're dead."

"I heard that rumor myself," answered Logan, "but when I checked it out I discovered it was some other guy."

*   *   *

Keyes and McMahon were rivals in a bitter election campaign. They decided to meet and agree on ground rules.

"Look," said Keyes, "we'll have to make this a clean campaign. For a start I'll promise to tell no more lies about you."

"Good," answered McMahon, "and I'll give you my solemn word not to tell the truth about you."

128

* * *

Horgan, a Dungannon resident was spouting off to a Dundalk friend, "Once they abolish hanging in this country they will have to hang twice as many."

* * *

"I want you to keep the suspect under constant surveillance," the Chief of Detectives told Donnelly, the new plainclothes man.

"Got you, Chief," said the Irishman. "And I'll keep an eye on him, too."

* * *

"Why in the name of Heaven," asked the weary passenger, "did they build the railway station three miles from the village?"

"Ah," nodded the porter, "they must have thought it would be a good thing to have it near the trains."

* * *

"Isn't it a pity that the Monahans have no children?"

"It is indeed, but I hear that sterility is hereditary on both sides of their family."

* * *

Two terrorists were on their way to plant a bomb. On the way they had to drive up a very bumpy road. "Go steady, Terry," said Mick, "we don't want the bomb to explode."

"Stop worrying, Mick. If it goes off, there's a spare in the trunk."

*   *   *

The battle raged since daylight and bullets flew from all sides. Tough Sgt. O'Reilly was not going to allow his men to retreat.

"Stay here," he shouted, "and keep firing even if you run out of ammunition!"

*   *   *

Mrs. Mahone spent her first vacation visiting Jerusalem. Impressed by its holy places, she turned to another tourist and asked, "Where will you find a modern building that has lasted as long as these ancient ones?"

*   *   *

Shannon returned home after his first holiday abroad and he didn't look too happy.

"Did you enjoy yourself?" asked his neighbor.

"Well to tell you the truth, I'm so glad to be home I'm not sorry I went."

*   *   *

"Dobie, will you hurry up," shouted his wife. "Haven't you an appointment with Quigley?"

"I have, but I told him I'd be late so I've lots of time yet."

*   *   *

O'Hara, a contestant on a TV quiz show was asked by the M.C., "What is the difference between an explosion and a collision?"

"In a collision," replied the Irishman, "there you are, but in an explosion where are you?"

*　　*　　*

"Aloysius, your uncle is on the phone and he wants to know if the new child is a boy or a girl."

"Well, now, will you ask the poor bothered man what else it could have been?"

*　　*　　*

Edith's Father: Do you think you could support my daughter if you married her?
Kendrick: Yes sir.
Edith's Father: Have you ever seen her eat?
Kendrick: Yes sir.
Edith's Father: Have you ever seen her eat when there's nobody looking?

*　　*　　*

Rattigan's employees were about to unionize. He stood before them and bellowed, "You are standing on the edge of a precipice that will be a weight on your necks all the rest of your days. You are a disgrace to the colors you are flying under."

*　　*　　*

Sgt. Shaughnessy noticed a soldier was wearing new-looking boots and was limping.

"Are your boots hurting you?" asked the sergeant.

"Yes, sir," replied the soldier.

"Every good soldier should wear his boots for a while before he puts them on," suggested the Irishman.

* * *

Maid: I'm sorry, but she said to tell you that she is not at home.

Quinn: Oh, that's all right, just tell her that I'm glad I didn't come.

* * *

O'Flynn was visited by his nephew, who told him that he had just entered the seminary. "That's fine," spoke up the uncle. "I'm glad to hear it. Make the most of your time and abilities, and I hope I shall live to hear you preach my funeral sermon!"

* * *

Reardon raised his fist and shouted. "I hate you, Hallahan, and believe me the sooner I never see your ugly face again, the better it will be for both of us when we meet again."

* * *

While impatiently waiting for a table in a restaurant, Mrs. Kiernan turned to another woman and said, "If they weren't so crowded here all the time, they'd do a lot more business."

* * *

Flanagan (*instructing new switchboard operator in answering techniques for the telephone*):

> When the bell rings you take up the receiver, place it to your ear and you will hear a voice saying "Hello. Are you there?" You will then answer "Yes" or "No" as the case may be.

* * *

"Well, listen," griped O'Leary, "if I called the wrong number, why did you answer the phone?"

* * *

"If you don't receive this letter, write and let me know."

—Obadiah Bull

* * *

"It's a great pleasure to be alone," reflected Eamon, "especially when Brigette is with me."

* * *

Perhaps one of the best bulls ever uttered was not spoken by an Irishman. On a *60 Minutes* TV program, film writer/director Billy Wilder quoted the legendary Jewish movie mogul Sam Goldwyn as saying, "If people don't go see a picture—nobody can stop them."

* * *

My Dearest Coreen,

I met you last night and you never came. Next time I'll meet you again whether you come or not. If I am there first, I'll write my name on the gatepost to let you know; and if it's you that's first, rub out my name and nobody will be any the wiser.

Darling Coreen, I would climb the highest mountain for your sake, and swim the widest sea. I would endure any hardships and suffer any trial to spend a moment by your side.

Your own ever loving Pat.

P.S. I'll be over to see you on Friday night if it's not raining.

* * *

"Women," claimed O'Loughlin, "are mighty similar in one way—there's no two of them alike."

* * *

Daley was invited to participate in his first fox hunt. He turned up wearing only one spur.

"Listen," said a friend, "you're only wearing one spur."

"Only one is needed," said Daley. "If one side of the horse goes the other is sure to follow along."

*　　*　　*

During the Vietnam War, Pvt. O'Keefe became annoyed by the nagging letters he received from his wife. One day he wrote back, "Please stop writing me any more letters. Let me enjoy this war in peace."

*　　*　　*

Mrs. Powell joined a group of people waiting for a bus and asked, "Has the next bus gone yet?"

*　　*　　*

Campbell was visiting McClannahan at the seashore. At breakfast on the first day Campbell said, "I got up at the crack of dawn today to see the sunrise over the ocean."

"Yes," said his host, "you couldn't have picked a better time to see it."

*　　*　　*

"A man is of little use when his wife is a widow."

—Obadiah Bull

*   *   *

Spinelli, an experienced hunter, took his friend Clusky, who had never gone hunting before, out in the woods and agreed to let him have the first shot. As they walked along, a rabbit suddenly jumped from the grass at their feet, ran through the bushes and disappeared. But Clusky failed to fire.

"Why didn't you shoot?" demanded Spinelli.

"Bejabbers," said the Irishman. "It was so sudden, I didn't see him until he was out of sight."

Joy Juice Jollies

At a wake Cassidy stumbled over to the host and gurgled, "Listen, thish punch is gettin' awful weak, f'r some reashun or n'other."

"Be careful there," came the reply. "You're dipping your cup into the goldfish bowl."

*   *   *

"Was that home brew of McNulty's very potent?"

"I don't know how potent it was, but during the evening McNulty tried to get inside his grandfather's clock, with the idea of phoning his wife that he wouldn't be home on time."

```
*      *      *
```

Bartender:	Here, you haven't paid for that whiskey you ordered.
Cavanaugh:	What's that you say? Hic!
Bartender:	I said you haven't paid for that whiskey you ordered.
Cavanaugh:	Did you pay for it? Hic!
Bartender:	Of course I did!
Cavanaugh:	Well, then, what's the good of both of us payin' for it? Hic!

```
*      *      *
```

"You say that Flanagan bet the boys down at the office $20 he could drink six bottles of his own homebrew at one sitting?"

"Yep. That was the bet."

"Who won?"

"Oh, Flanagan won the money all right, but he lost the homebrew."

```
*      *      *
```

Back in the days of the Old West an Irish laborer used to come into a saloon, see a customer lying helpless on the sawdust floor, point to him, and say, "Gimme some of that."

```
*      *      *
```

The owner of Toohey's Tavern had a great sense of humor. To have fun with his tipsy customers he created a "Ghost" cocktail.

Toohey pours into a trick shaker five or six colorful liquids and shakes them vigorously. When he upends the shaker, not a drop comes out. Then he says, "Drink this down, and the chances are you'll disappear yourself."

One night Finnegan staggered into the tavern and lifted the empty glass and Toohey tried it on him. He took a hefty swig, and said, "Pfui! Too sweet!"

* * *

Caddigan left the Poteen Convention at 3:30 a.m., and was taken to his doorstep by a considerate taxi driver at 3:58. He had almost made it to the bedroom when his wife's prized cuckoo clock sounded four times. Caddigan cuckooed four more times, called out, "Heigh ho, it's off to work I go!" and quickly left the house.

That night Mrs. Caddigan said, "I've decided to get rid of that cuckoo clock. Last night it cuckooed four times, tripped over a chair, said 'damn it,' then cuckooed four times more!"

* * *

After a joyous liquid meeting of the Hibernian Society in South Boston, several members staggered up West Broadway late one night. They stopped in front of a large Victorian house. After much discussion, Desmond advanced and pounded on the door. A woman stuck her head out of a second-story window and demanded, "What is it?"

"Ish thish the residence of Mr. O'Callahan?" asked Desmond.

"It is. What do you want?"

"Ish it possible I have the honor of speakin' to Misshus O'Callahan?"

"Yes. What do you want?"

"Dear Misshus O'Callahan! Good Misshus O'-Callahan. Will you—hic!—come down an' pick out Mister O'Callahan? The rest of us want to go home."

*   *   *

Reformer: Young man, do you realize that you will never get anywhere by drinking?

Fennelly: Ain't it the truth? I've started home from this corner five times already.

*   *   *

A buxom young colleen from Derry,
On ale was loving and merry,
   She dallied with sin,
   On vodka and gin,
But was rigid and frigid on sherry.

*   *   *

Kathleen came home from college and announced, to her mother, "I've got a case of VD."

"Well," said the Irish woman, "put it in the cellar, your father'll drink anything."

*   *   *

"I see that McCullen has quit drinking."

"That so?"

"Yes. He fell out of a window on the tenth floor while he was drunk, and he hasn't taken a drop since."

*   *   *

MacNamara sauntered into a saloon, banged on the bar, and said: "A double J & B. I need it. It's gonna be a terrible fight."

The bartender served him his drink. Mac-Namara polished it off and shouted, "Anybody here a doctor?" When someone admitted he was, the Irishman said, "Stick around, doc, you'll be needed. It's gonna be a bloody fight." Then he said to the bartender, "Another scotch. Make it a triple. I'm gonna need it, believe me. This fight is gonna be one of the worst."

He finished the triple and asked if there was an undertaker in the house. A man rose and said, "I'm an undertaker."

"Don't go 'way, mister," shouted MacNamara. "There's gonna be a job for you soon. It's gonna be a helluva terrible fight." MacNamara then said to the bartender, "Gimme four triples in a row. I need 'em bad. What an awful fight it's gonna be."

"Say," asked the bartender, "Who you going to fight with, mister?"

"You," said the Irishman. "I ain't got no money to pay for the drinks."

* * *

Walsh: But judge, I wasn't drunk.
Judge: The officer says you were trying to climb a lamp post.
Walsh: I was, judge. A couple of crocodiles kept followin' me 'round, and I don't mind tellin' you they were gettin' on me nerves.

A policeman walking his beat one night in Brooklyn came upon an unusual sight. McInnerny, totally tanked up, was down on his knees beneath a street lamp peering at the sidewalk.

"What's the matter," inquired the cop. "Lose something?"

"Yup. Ish awful tough. I jusht losht a half dollar."

"Too bad. How did it happen?"

"Hole in my pocket," said McInnerny, "ish awful tough."

"Did you first miss it right around here?"

"No. I losht it down on the next street."

"Then what are you looking around here for?"

"The light ish better at thish corner," said the Irishman.

146

It was past midnight when Donovan began banging on the door of a house in Denver. An upstairs window opened and a little man shouted down, "What the devil do you want?"

Donavan belched some beer gas and said, "Shay, are you Professor Harris the Zoologist?"

"Yes, what do you want at this time of night?"

"Are you the Professor Harris who advertised for a man to go with you to Africa to capture lions?"

"I'm the man."

"Well, I jush came around to tell you that I couldn't go."

* * *

SKIBBEREEN SONNET

Thirsty days hath September,
April, June and November;
All the rest are thirsty too,
Except for him who hath home brew.

* * *

Nora: You've been drinking. I can smell it on your breath.

Sean: Not a drop. I've been eating frogs' legs. What you smell is the hops.

* * *

"Does McGinty drink much?"

"Drink? If he died and was reincarnated he'd come back as a bar sponge."

* * *

Faherty was passing a house at 3:00 A.M. when he noticed a man leaning against the doorway. "What's the matter?" he asked. "Are you drunk?"

"Yeah," he answered.

"Shall I help you upstairs?"

"Yeah."

So Faherty half-carried the helpless one to the second floor, opened the first door he came to and pushed him in. When Faherty reached the ground floor again, he found another drunk in a worse condition than the first. "Are you drunk, too?" he asked.

"Yeah," replied the other feebly.

"Want me to take you upstairs, too?"

"Yeah."

So Faherty dragged him to the second floor, opened the first door and showed him in. When the Irishman came down the third time, he saw still another drunk. Faherty was just going to offer his service again, when the man lurched out into the street and screamed to a passing police car, "Please, Officer, protect me from this man. He keeps carrying me upstairs and throwing me down the elevator shaft!"

* * *

Kernan and McNutt, friends from the old sod, met in Copley Square and decided to hoist a few in a nearby bar.

"Have you ever tried usin' horseradish in yer whisky?" asked Kernan.

"It gives the stuff a grand sparkle."

So, on the next round they gingerly sprinkled their glasses with horseradish.

After draining his glass Kernan began to weep.

"What are yer cryin' for?" asked McNutt.

"I'm cryin' 'cause me old father was hanged. And it was he who taught me to use horseradish in my whisky."

McNutt belted down his drink and began to sob uncontrollably.

"And what are you cryin' for?" asked Kernan.

"I'm cryin'," said McNutt, " 'cause you weren't hanged with your father."

* * *

In Boston at eight o'clock one Sunday morning Gilfoyle was clinging to a lamp post, he was the victim of his usual Saturday night celebration.

A man approached him and said, "Can you tell me where the Fourth Presbyterian Church is?"

"Mishter," replied the Irishman, "I don't even know where th' first one ish!"

* * *

Did you hear about the Irishman who was picked up for drunkenness?

At the police station he was allowed one phone call—so he called the liquor store.

* * *

SIGN ON WINDOW OF BRANIGAN'S BAR

We accept resignations
from Alcoholics Anonymous

* * *

McClosky had been ill many times over the years. Sometimes he would actually cease breathing and appear totally lifeless. But the Irishman always regained consciousness. One night after he had come out of a state of coma, his friend Gilooley said to him, "And how'll we know when ye're dead? Ye're after wakin' up every toime."

"Bring me a glass of whiskey," replied McClosky, "and say to me, 'Here's to ye, Mac,' and if I don't rise and drink, then bury me."

* * *

Hennilly: I shay—hic—all these girls have got awful broad belts on.
McCarthy: Belts! (hic) Them's dresses.

* * *

Gallagher was old, and he had a wooden leg,
And he hobbled all about on this artificial peg.
He hobbled to a bar—this was many moons
        ago—
And he stayed there longer than he'd really
        ought, you know.

In the wee small hours he tried hard to travel
        home,
All unsteady on his legs and bewildered in his
        dome;
But he hadn't got far when his solid maple pin
Struck a hole in the sidewalk and slipped right
        in.

Yes, it slipped right in, and it stuck right tight,
And the old Irishman's limb was anchored for
        the night.
Did he holler for help? He assuredly did not.
For he never knew what happened, this befud-
        dled old sot.

But he hobbled right on with his one good
        prop,
And he never stopped to think, and he never
        thought to stop.
And his wooden limb still stuck right tight.
And he walked around himself the whole damn
        night.

"What sort of a part does Mahoney take in the play?"

"A very difficult part. In the last act he has to refuse a drink."

*　　*　　*

Crandall, a confirmed drunk, stood on a street corner in dire need of a nip. Just then a hearse made a sudden stop and the dead man it was carrying slid out the rear door. When the hearse moved on, Crandall picked up the body, dragged it into Sullivan's saloon and leaned it up against the bar.

Sullivan asked for orders and Crandall requested two scotches. After he'd knocked those off, he ordered two more. When they were consumed the owner said, "That'll be $7."

"My friend'll take care of it," said Crandall, pointing to the body leaning over the bar, and left for the men's room.

"That'll cost you $7, buddy," said Sullivan to the corpse. When there was no reply, Sullivan lifted the man's head and began shaking it. "Look, fella, if you don't pay this bill I'm gonna bust you one with this bottle."

Not getting an answer, the Irishman shoved the dead man and the body fell to the floor. At that moment Crandall returned and began sobbing.

"Oh, my God! You killed my best friend!"

"I had to!" screamed Sullivan, "He pulled a knife on me!"

OVERHEARD IN TUMULTY'S TAVERN

"Whiskey may shorten your life, but you'll see twice as much in half the time."

"I only drink to forget and the only thing I forget is when to stop."

"Some Irishmen would live strictly on a liquid diet if it weren't for the pretzels and peanuts."

"I don't like to drink but I got a tape worm that's a lush."

"Some men are driven to drink, but I usually walk to the corner saloon."

"I had a great time at the last party, but I still don't know how I got ketchup stains on my socks."

"I've only had tee Martooneys and I'm not under the confluence of incohol as some thinkle peep. But the drunker I stand here, the longer I get."

Ed Scannel, the terrific Tempe, Arizona Conference Bureau Director, gets big titters with this rib tickler:

Mullawny, stewed to the gills, staggered through a cemetery one night. Looking for a short-cut to his house, he fell into an open grave that had been dug for a burial the next day.

Two hours later another drunk came wandering through the cemetery and heard Mullawny call up from below, "Hey, up there, help me, I'm freezing."

The good-hearted drunk called back, "No wonder you're cold. They forgot to cover you up!"

And he picked up a shovel and began filling up the grave.

SIGN IN CLANCY'S SALOON MEN'S ROOM

Whatsoever a man drinketh—
So shall he pee

*   *   *

McQuillan walked into a bar and ordered martini after martini, each time removing the olives and placing them in a jar. When the jar was filled with olives and the martinis all consumed, the Irishman started to leave.

"S'cuse me," said a customer who was puzzled over what McQuillan had done. "What was that all about?"

"Nothing," said the Irishman, "my wife just sent me out for a jar of olives."

*   *   *

Driscoll tottered out of a Toledo saloon and sat down on the curb under a lamp post. While urinating he fell asleep, and two pranksters tied a blue ribbon around his penis.

He woke up next morning, saw the ribbon, and said to his dong, "I don't know where you've been or what you've been doin', but I'm glad to see you won first prize."

*   *   *

In a small town in Northern Island, Kilgallen and his friend Griffith got drunk twice a week. These celebrations had taken place for thirty years, but then suddenly Griffith passed on. In the hope of getting her husband to quit the hard stuff Mrs. Kilgallen asked Father O'Hagen to scare him with some horrible pronouncement.

That evening the parish priest asked, "Do you know how your pal Griffith died?"

"No," answered a saddened Kilgallen.

"The whiskey had been taken into his circulation and so saturated his body that one night before going to bed, Griffith went to blow out a candle. His breath caught fire and he was cremated on the spot."

"Father, do you have a bible with yer?"

"I do," said the priest. "And what would you be needin' it for?"

"I'm gonna swear an oath," said Kilgallen, "from this time forward I'll never blow out a candle again as long as I live!"

Tipperary Toasts

Here's to good old whiskey,
    So amber and so clear;
'Tis not so sweet as woman's lips,
    But a damned sight more sincere.

       *   *   *

Here's to champagne, the drink divine,
    That makes us forget our troubles;
It's made of a dollar's worth of wine
    And three dollars' worth of bubbles.

       *   *   *

Here's to a temperance supper
    With water in glasses tall,
And coffee and tea to end with
    And me not there at all.

*　*　*

Drink to life and the passing show,
And the eyes of the prettiest girl you know.

*　*　*

Here's to the man who loves his wife,
    And loves his wife alone;
For many a man loves another man's wife
    When he might be loving his own.

*　*　*

Drink today and drown all sorrow;
You shall, perhaps, not do it tomorrow.

*　*　*

If all be true, as I do think,
There are five reasons we should drink:
    Good wine, a friend, or being dry,
    Or lest we should meet by and by,
Or any other reason why.

*　*　*

May the bloom of the face never extend to the
nose.

*　*　*

Here's to the lasses we've loved;
    Here's to the lips we've pressed;
For of kisses and lasses,
Like liquor in glasses,
    The last is always the best.

*   *   *

Here's to the girls who do,
    And here's to the girls who don't;
But damn the girls who say they will,
    And then decide they won't.

*   *   *

Here's to a short life but a merry one;
    And a quick death and an easy one;
A pretty girl and a loving one;
    A cold bottle and another one.

*   *   *

Here's to the man who takes a wife,
    Let him make no mistakes;
For there is a world of difference
    Whose wife it is he takes.

*   *   *

163

A dinner, coffee and cigars,
    Of friends, a half a score.
Each favorite vintage in its turn,
    What man could wish for more?

*   *   *

Here's to you as good as you are;
    And here's to me as bad as I am.
But as good as you are and as bad as I am,
    I'm as good as you are as bad as I am.

*   *   *

The miser may be pleased with gold,
    The sporting beau with a pretty lass;
But I'm best pleased when I behold
    The nectar sparkling in the glass.

*   *   *

Here's to the joke, the good old joke,
    The joke that our fathers told;
It is ready tonight and is jolly and bright
    As it was in the days of old.

*   *   *

Here's to the game of twenty toes,
    It's known all over town;
The women play it with ten toes up,
    And the men with ten toes down.

* * *

"Here's to the tailor's daughter. . . .
she's the only thing he ever made that fit me."

* * *

Here's to the ladies: First in our hearts and
first in our pocketbooks.

* * *

To our sweethearts and wives.
May they never meet!

* * *

Here's to the happiest hours of my life,
Spent in the arms of another man's wife:
    My mother!

* * *

Here's to matrimony, the high sea for which
no compass has yet been invented.

* * *

At last I've found the perfect wife,
    I could not ask for more.
She's deaf and dumb and oversexed
    And she owns a liquor store.

* * *

May you live as long as you want
And never want as long as you live.

*　　*　　*

May you die in bed at 95 years—
Shot by a jealous husband.

*　　*　　*

May you live to be a hundred years—
With one extra year to repent.

*　　*　　*

May the road rise to meet you
May the wind be always at your back
    The sunshine warm upon your face
    The rain fall soft upon your fields
And until we meet again
May God hold you in the hollow of His hand.

*　　*　　*

Health and long life to you
The wife of your choice to you
    A child every year to you
    Land without rent to you
And may you be half-an-hour in heaven
Before the devil knows you're dead!

*　　*　　*

Here is champagne to our real friends
And a real pain to your sham friends.

* * *

May the frost never afflict your spuds
May the outside leaves of your cabbage
     Always be free from worms
May the crows never pick your haystack
     And may your donkey always be in foal.

* * *

The health of the salmon to you:
A long life,
A full heart
And a wet mouth.

* * *

Here's a toast to great ambition,
     About which people rant.
It makes you want to do the thing
     That everyone knows you can't.

* * *

Here's to our fisherman bold;
     Here's to the fish he caught;
Here's to the ones that got away,
     And here's to the ones he bought.

* * *

Saint Patrick was a gentleman,
Who, thro' strategy and stealth,
    Drove all the snakes from Ireland,
    Here's a bumper to his health.
But not too many bumpers,
Lest we lose ourselves, and then
    Forget the good Saint Patrick,
    And see the snakes again.

Shamrock Shenanigans

Fogarty was continually late for work, so one night he went to bed early and had a sound sleep. When he arrived at the office he said to the boss, "Well, I'm early for a change."

"Yes," said the boss, "but where were you yesterday?"

*　　*　　*

O'Dell went into the Post Office to mail a letter.

"This letter is too heavy," said the clerk, "you'll have to put more stamps on it."

"Won't that just make it heavier?" asked the Irishman.

169

*   *   *

Corrigan and Sheehan were doing a crossword puzzle together. One clue read: "Old MacDonald had a . . ."

After a little while Corrigan said, "I think I've got it—it's 'farm.' "

"That might be right," said Sheehan, "but how do you spell it?"

"I know that too," said Corrigan. "E-I-E-I-O."

*   *   *

Farmer Moynihan was walking along a country road carrying a sack over his shoulder. O'Sheel hailed him and asked "What've you got in the sack?"

"Got some chickens," replied Moynihan.

"If I can guess how many are in there, can I have one of them?"

"If you can guess how many are in there, you can have both of them," said the Irish farmer.

*   *   *

Foreman: (*to Finley loitering on job*): What are you doing here?
Finley: Nothing.
Foreman: (*to Mulroy*) And what are you doing?
Mulroy: Giving him a hand.

*   *   *

How does an Irishman cope with a gas leak?
He puts a bucket underneath it.

*　　*　　*

McBride was telling Ferguson that he had just heard a new Irish joke.

"It's about an Irishman who tried to sell an American tourist two skulls of the Duke of York; one of the Duke of York as an adult and the other of the Duke of York as a boy," he told him.

"It sounds as if it's a very funny joke," said Ferguson, "how does it go?"

*　　*　　*

The Irish invented garbage disposals long before Americans. They had them fully nine hundred years ago. They were called "Windows."

*　　*　　*

Belson, a Seattle banker, asked Corrigan, his new Irish servant, "Did you mail that important letter I gave you?"

"I did indeed," said the Irishman.

"Then how come you brought back the money I gave you for the stamp?"

"I didn't have to use it," said Corrigan, "I slipped the letter into the box when nobody was looking."

*　　*　　*

Duane Vail, Gualala, California's dynamo druggist, donated this dazzler:

Doheny, a giant of a man, landed a job as a deep-sea diver. They handed him a pick and told him he'd need it. Then they adjusted his helmet and lowered him into the water. After a few moments, the man on top received the signal to haul him to the surface.

After he removed Doheny's helmet he asked, "My God, what's the matter?"

"I quit," declared the Irishman. "I can niver woork with a pick when I can't spit on me hands."

Did you hear about the Irishman who couldn't understand how he had only three brothers when his sisters had four?

*   *   *

Kerrigan became a bank robber but didn't do too well. On his first job he said to the bank teller, "Hand over all your money."

"I won't," said the teller, "but I'll tell you what, just to show there's no hard feelings, I'll give you $500 for your gun."

And he did.

*   *   *

How do you recognize an Irish explorer?

Look in his back pack for the package of dehydrated water.

*   *   *

Did you hear about the Irishman who bought washable wallpaper?

He'd only washed it twice when it was stolen from his clothesline.

*   *   *

Then there was the Irishman who thought that Hertz Van Rentals was a famous Dutch painter.

*   *   *

A colleen who lived in Newbliss,
Would stand on her head for a kiss,
    When people asked why,
    She replied, cute and sly,
I like to give head when like this.

*   *   *

Higgins: I read once where John McCormack,
            the grand Irish tenor, learned to sing
            with a mouth full of pebbles.
O'Casey: So?
Higgins: When I was a boy I practiced in the
            same way.
O'Casey: An' what happened?
Higgins: One day I got the hiccups and broke
            fourteen windows!

*   *   *

O'Toole became rich despite the lack of an education. And despite his financial success he remained as unsophisticated and prudish as a Galway nun. Now on his deathbed he said to the priest, "I'm leavin' half me fortune to the church and the other half to the state college."

"Devil's work!" cried the priest. "That college takes decent boys and girls and make them matriculate together. They even have to use the same curriculum!"

The bequest to the college was cancelled.

*   *   *

O'Houlihan believed that when the refrigerator door was closed the little light didn't go out. He continually sneaked up on the fridge hoping to prove this, but as soon as the door closed he could no longer see inside.

One day his pal McGraw suggested that he actually go inside a fridge and see for himself.

When O'Houlihan was locked inside the fridge McGraw decided to go for a quick whiskey but after a few drinks he forgot all about his friend. He returned three hours later and released O'Houlihan who was frozen stiff.

"Well," asked McGraw, "did the little light go out?"

"I don't know," said O'Houlihan. "It was so dark in there I couldn't see a damn thing."

*   *   *

Did you hear about the Irishman who took his tie back to the store because it was too tight?

*   *   *

Mrs. McGonigle and Mrs. Culhane were boasting about their children.

"My little fellow is only ten," said Mrs. McGonigle, "and he has read all Shakespeare's plays."

"That's nothing," said the other Irishwoman, "my little lad read them in the original Greek when he was only eight."

*   *   *

Hart: I think we met at this hotel last year. Your overcoat looks familiar to me.

Ryan: But I didn't have this coat then.

Hart: I know. I did.

*   *   *

A neurotic girl from Kilbane,
Once screwed every man on a train.
    Saying, "My nerves it'll cure,
    But can I endure,
The boredom of being too sane?"

*   *   *

Kildare had just arrived in England and was asked if he had travelled by boat or plane.

"I don't know," said the Irishman, "my brother bought the tickets."

*   *   *

McDermott and Garrigan were building a 600 foot chimney. Just as they were putting the final brick in place one of them happened to glance at the plans.

"You fool," exclaimed McDermott, "you've been reading these plans upside down. We were supposed to be building a well."

*   *   *

McCroy was out digging his garden one day, when he saw a little creature at his feet. He lifted his shovel up to kill it, but to his surprise it spoke. "Wait, I'm a leprechaun. Spare my life and I'll grant ye three wishes."

"Three wishes?" said the Irishman. "Well, Oi'm tirsty from all dis digging, Oi'd like a bottle o' cold Guinness."

The leprechaun snapped his fingers, and McCroy was holding a bottle of Guinness.

"That bottle," said the leprechaun, "is a magic bottle. It'll never empty—it'll pour forever."

McCroy took a swig. Lovely.

"What are your next two wishes," asked the leprechaun.

"Oi tink Oi'd like two more o' dese, please."

178

Dealey was found wandering around Dublin wearing nothing except a blanket. When arrested he explained to the Desk Sergeant.

"I was out walking with a girl in the woods and she told me to take off all my clothes and go to town. So here I am."

* * *

Mrs. Connelly, Mrs. Carey and Mrs. McCroy, three housewives, were gossiping on a Staten Island stoop. A down-on-his-luck bum came by and asked for a meal. Mrs. Connelly and Carey refused, but Mrs. McCroy invited him in the house.

As she prepared the food in the oven she kept bending over, and the sight of her rear aroused the bum. He got an erection which sneaked out of a hole in his pants. But he pushed it back. Then his member popped out of another hole in his pants and he shoved it back. This happened several times until Mrs. McCroy fed him and he left.

She went back out on the sidewalk where the other two women looked at her with shame.

"Listen," said she, "I admit he was a ragged, dirty bum, but he had five or six of the greatest peckers you ever saw."

* * *

Did you hear about the Irishman who stayed up all night to see where the sun went?

It finally dawned on him.

*   *   *

Mrs. Kilkenny sat in Dr. Riley's office. "I'm kinda embarrassed to tell you me problem," said the middle-aged woman.

"Now, just relax. I'm here to help you," said the physician. "What seems to be the trouble?"

"In the mornin' when I have to pee it comes out nickels."

"Yes?" said the M.D.

"Then in the afternoon I pee dimes."

"Uh huh?"

"And at night before I go to bed I pee quarters," said Mrs. Kilkenny. "What in heaven's name do you think it is?"

"My dear, you've got nothing to worry about. You're just going through the change."

*   *   *

O'Shea was playing solitaire while his neighbor Lohan looked on. After a while Lohan said, "Hey you're cheatin' yourself."

O'Shea put his finger on his lips and said: "Shh . . . Don't speak too loud. For years I've been cheatin' meself."

"And did you never catch yourself cheatin'?"

"No. I'm much too smart for that."

*   *   *

181

Michael Gates, the Sea Ranch super real estate salesman, gets smiles with this silly snapper:

O'Myer, a plumber, was summoned to a large Bel Air mansion to repair a leak in the drawing room. O'Myer was admitted by the butler who cautioned, "You be careful of the floors. They have just been polished."

"They's no danger of me slippin' on them," replied the Irishman. "I have spikes in me shoes."

*   *   *

Mrs. Flanigan finished her lunch of corned beef and a large helping of cabbage and went shopping at Gimbels. She got in the elevator and suddenly expelled a very loud and large amount of gas.

The man standing next to her exclaimed, "Lady, did you just fart?"

"Well," said the Irish woman, "you don't think I smell like that all the time!"

*   *   *

Mrs. Bryant and Mrs. Keenan entered a grocery store. Mrs. Bryant ordered everything that was on the shelves. When the counter couldn't hold any more, the clerk said, "Where do you want this delivered?"

"No place!" snickered the Irish woman. "I just wanted to show me friend Mrs. Keenan here how much stuff you could buy for two dollars before the second World War."

*   *   *

IRISH GENTLEMAN

One who never strikes a lady without provocation

*   *   *

Did you hear about the Irishman who was practicing to become a part-time surgeon?

He bought an anatomy book and took its appendix out.

* * *

Healy was taking a walk when he found a small mirror lying on the ground. He picked it up, looked at it and said:

"What an ugly picture. No wonder whoever owned it threw it away."

* * *

Two Irishmen were applying for jobs.

Personnel Director: Your name?
First Irishman: James Damnit Monagan.
Personnel Director: Damnit! That's a peculiar name.
First Irishman: Yes. The priest burnt his finger with the candle while baptising me.
Personnel Director: And your name?
Second Irishman: Walter Damnit Again McKee . . . same priest.

* * *

185

O'Ryan left Ireland to try his luck in the United States.

Before getting on the ship, he was stopped by a gray-haired woman. "I have a son in America," she said, "he lives in a little white house in Connecticut. I haven't heard from him in 15 years. If you meet, please tell him to write his poor old mother. His name is Dunn."

O'Ryan landed in New York and a few months later took the bus up to Connecticut. O'Ryan said to the driver, "Would you let me off in front of the *little white house*."

The driver, thinking O'Ryan needed to relieve himself, dropped him in front of a park. O'Ryan spotted the park attendant. "Could you be tellin' me where to find the *little white house*?"

The attendant, certain he meant the men's room, replied, "Go down this lane and turn left!"

The immigrant followed directions, thrilled that at last he would find Dunn. Just as he got to the *little white house* a man came out zipping up his fly.

"Are you Dunn?" asked O'Ryan.

"Yeah!" said the man.

"Then why don't you write your poor old mother in Ireland?"

*   *   *

Darren: Everything that Flanagan touches turns to gold.

Agnes: I wish he'd touch this watch you gave me.

*   *   *

186

McComb awoke one night and heard a noise under his bed.

Fearing that there might be a burglar there, he cried out "Is anybody there?"

"No," said the burglar.

"That's funny," said the Irishman, "I could have sworn I heard a noise."

*   *   *

O'Howan and his wife were on a cruise around the Greek Isles.

"Did you hand over your jewels to the ship's purser for safekeeping like I told you?" he asked her on their first day out.

"I didn't have to, darlin', " she replied, "there was a lovely little wall safe in my cabin called a porthole."

*   *   *

Mulligan got lost while on a hunting trip, and was found by some monks who took him to their monastery and nursed him back to health. When he got well he noticed that all they ate at the monastery was fish and chips.

Mulligan decided to thank the chef for his good food and walked into the kitchen. He said "Hello, are you the fish fryer?"

"No, I'm the chip monk."

*   *   *

McCarran and Houlihan were crossing a bridge over the river. They noticed a man leaning over the parapet holding a girl by the ankles. Her head and shoulders were in the water.

"What're doin'?" asked McCarran.

"We're fishing," said the man.

"How could you fish like that?" asked Houlihan.

"Well," said the man, "my wife waits for a fish to come by. As it passes she tickles its tummy, giving a slight jerk of her left leg as she does it. I pull her up quickly and there she is with a fish."

McCarran and Houlihan thought the guy was putting them on but suddenly the girl's ankle twitched and up she came clutching a big brown trout to her bosom.

The Irishmen were flabbergasted and decided to try it themselves. They rushed off, found a bridge and McCarran quickly lowered Houlihan over the side.

In a minute Houlihan's leg twitched. McCarran said, "Have yeh a fish?"

"No," shouted Houlihan, "there's a damn train comin'."

189

During the days of the draft McCormick received his notice and was told to bring a urine sample to the Selective Service Headquarters.

Figuring on outfoxing the draft board, the Irishman filled a bottle with urine from his father, girlfriend, and dog, and then added some of his own. After turning in the sample, McCormick waited for about a half hour.

Finally the lab technician came out. "According to our lab tests," he reported, "your father has diabetes, your girlfriend is pregnant, your dog is in heat, and you're in the army."

*   *   *

Private: Do you know what the good-looking blonde said to the lieutenant?
Sergeant: No.
Private: That's right.

*   *   *

Private: Do you know what the good looking blonde said to the lieutenant?
Sergeant: What, again?
Private: That's right.

*   *   *

Master Sergeant Penrod and his wife were coming from a N.C.O. dance and were challenged by Pvt. MacAndrew, the sentry, as they approached the guard room.

"Halt. Who goes there?" challenged MacAndrew.

"Oh, Jesus, Mary and Joseph," exclaimed the startled wife.

"Advance, Holy Family, to be recognized," replied the Irishman.

*　　*　　*

Private:　Do you know what the good-looking blonde said to the lieutenant?
Sergeant:　You've tried that twice already.
Private:　That's right.

*　　*　　*

Did you hear about the Irishman who had his sundial floodlit?

He wanted to be able to tell the time at night.

*　　*　　*

A contest was held recently in Ireland to predict the score in the All-Ireland football final.

First prize was two tickets for the match.

*　　*　　*

Phelps was playing his ukulele in the middle of Boyleston Street.

"Have you a permit to play your ukelele in the middle of the street?" asked a policeman.

"I'm afraid I haven't," said Phelps.

"Then I shall have to ask you to accompany me," said the officer.

"All right," said the Irishman. "What do you want to sing?"

*   *   *

Killoran got a job in the vegetable department of the neighborhood supermarket and on his first day got a chance to display typical Irish ingenuity. A man walked up to him and said, "I'd like to buy half a head of lettuce."

"I'm sorry, mista," said Killoran, "we only sell a whole head of lettuce."

"You don't understand," said the customer. "I'm going to a party and I only need a half a head."

"I just told you sir, we don't sell them by halves."

"Why don't you go back and ask the manager."

Not knowing the man was following him, Killoran marched into the rear of the store and shouted to the produce manager, "Hey Harry, some jackass wants to buy a half a head of lettuce." Then Killoran spotted the customer behind and added, "And this nice man wants to buy the other half."

* * *

What's the biggest educational problem in Ireland?

Kindergarten dropout.

* * *

Mularkey the mortician was asked, "How is business?"

"Terrible," he replied, "I haven't buried a living soul for over a month."

* * *

O'Nolan was talking to a rare book collector.

"It's funny I should meet you," he told him, "because only last week I threw away an old book, a bible printed by some fellow with a name like Guten . . ."

"Oh my God," gasped the book collector, "It wasn't Gutenberg by any chance was it?"

"That was it exactly," said O'Nolan. "Gutenberg was his name."

"Do you know," said the collector, "that the last Gutenberg bible that came on the market sold for over a million dollars?"

"Ah, mine wouldn't have been worth anything," said the Irishman. "Some fellow called Martin Luther had scribbled his name all over it."

* * *

WILDE ON WILDE

I love humor. I've spent over 30 years studying, analyzing, researching, teaching, performing and writing it. The fascination started in Jersey City where I was born in 1928. I grew up during the great Depression and along with scratching to make a buck, making jokes was a way of life. (To survive in an Irish neighborhood a Jewish boy quickly learns to keep his playmates laughing.)

After a two year stint in the Marine Corps where I found I could make leathernecks laugh, I worked my way through the University of Miami, Florida doing a comedy act at the beach hotels. When I graduated I entertained in night clubs and hotels all over America. I got to play Vegas and Tahoe and the other big-time spots being the "supporting" comedian for Ann-Margret, Debbie Reynolds, Pat Boone and a whole lot more.

I've done acting roles on *Mary Tyler Moore*, *Rhoda*, *Sanford and Son* and other sitcoms; performed on Carson, Griffin, Douglas and did a bunch of TV commercials.

This is my 26th "Official" Joke Book. I'm also proud of the two serious works I've done on comedy technique: *The Great Comedians Talk About Comedy* and *How The Great Comedy Writers Create Laughter*. Both books have been called the "definitive" works on the subject.

My books have sold over 6,000,000 which makes them the largest selling humor series in publishing history. And while I'm blowing my own horn here, the best thing I ever did was to marry Maryruth Poulos from Wyoming. We live in California in an Irish neighborhood and I'm still trying to make my neighbors laugh.